T.G.I.F.

A Girls' Guide to Making Cocktails

by Karen Ellingson Hinds

ISBN: 1480087092
ISBN-13: 9781480087095

I would like to dedicate this book to my late father who was my biggest fan, to my mother, who tirelessly and unselfishly devoted her entire life to my sister and me, and, taught us that we could do whatever we set our minds to do; to my sister, who made growing up fun and to my husband and taste-tester-in-chief who encouraged me to finish this book and always believed in me.

Contents

Acknowledgements

The Grande Dame of thank you's goes to my husband for allowing me to transform our kitchen into a "cocktail lab" for weeks on end and for putting up with all the mason jars that occupied the refrigerator. (*Eventually they were replaced for food!*)

Thank you to all of my friends that let me experiment on you.

Kalene, you're the best. I don't think we could have laughed any harder if we tried. You're my encyclopedia of music knowledge, my girlfriend that's always up for a "dance-off", and, who has a personality that sparkles as much as your jewelry box. My bourbon buddy Sam, who gave it to me straight when I made some doozies one night at a taste-fest, and, my friend Bob who's always up for tasting whatever I feel like throwing in the shaker.

Jennifer, you rock. The illustration you designed for my cover is absolutely perfect. Your ability to understand my vision and cracking my "you know", "kind of like this, but not like that" code was amazing. Our cocktail infused design meetings were always a hoot. Thank you. Tim, I had a blast shooting pictures with you. You have such a precise eye, crafty way and are a master of lighting. I just love you!

Liz, I appreciate your friendship. Your kind words, generosity and always fun happy hours inspire me. Mom, thank you for your continued support and help with editing.

Introduction

Girlfriends,

I dedicate this book to you. This book represents my passion for entertaining, the love I have for my friends and the curiosity I have for making cocktails in non-conventional ways. (I also love pretty glassware).

Living in San Francisco exposed my palette to what I would call a culinary theme park. Outstanding food, great wine and crafted cocktails like I'd never experienced. I became fascinated with the mindset and confidence of a skilled bartender, studying how they would think, muddle, mix, shake, strain, pour and twist their cocktails. It was like watching liquid art flow into the perfect glass.

Some bars looked more like science labs with beakers filled with homemade bitters, apothecary jars filled with house infused spirits and various ice machines that housed different shapes of ice cubes. (Size matters!)

From that point on, wherever I traveled I paid special attention to the bartender. I like to sit at the bar, order "off the menu" and watch my drink come to life.

In writing this book, I also realized that life is a lot like a cocktail. Sometimes it's on the rocks and sometimes it's served straight up with a twist (if we're lucky). Thanks to getting temporarily stuck in my pants this summer, I realized that if I could wiggle my way out of a pair of wool, skinny leg dress pants with the zipper in the back, without any collateral damage, I most certainly could finish this book!

I'm not kidding. I paid too much to cut them off, I didn't know the guy across the street well enough to ask him for a hand and I was too embarrassed to call my husband at work. So, I sucked it in and shimmied my way out of them.

It's kind of ironic that I would write a cocktail book. Actually, it's ironic for two reasons. One, I hated writing class in school. Two, I was raised in a very non-alcoholic family. (Go figure!)

Growing up, I wasn't into drinking at all. I played basketball in school, and when I wasn't doing that, I liked dancing and just hanging out with my friends.

My real initiation into the cocktail world (and, only the second time I had anything other than a Bud or wine cooler to drink) was when I started dating what I call the "Dynasty" family. Remember that show?

They had a beautiful house situated on a private lake and a well stocked bar with monogrammed glasses, Baccarat crystal and high-end spirits.

They served drinks before, after, and during everything, "tink-tink, time for oysters on the half shell" would be the call after a sunny day on the lake. Then, we'd start placing our cocktail order with the head cheese of the house.

Being as though I was basically a cocktail virgin, I asked for a recommendation as to what to drink. The head cheese said I would enjoy a gin and tonic. Okay then! My cocktail arrived on a small white linen napkin with a tiny monogram in the corner. He was right. It was delicious.

Just before dinner another "call out", "would everyone start taking your seats please"? It was time to head to the formal dining room for dinner. There was so much glassware on the table it looked like a dime toss booth at the state fair! (A lot more classy of course). There I sat like a deer in the head-lights with a full ensemble of goblets flanking both sides of my dinner plate. Back in the day I read Emily Post's book on etiquette but now it was time to dip into my memory bank and try not to make an ass of myself.

In my house it was easy. One glass for milk and one for water.

Have you ever thought of your personality like a cocktail? Here is mine.

High ball, low ball, glass half empty, glass half full, no excuses is how I roll.

1 part origination
1 part imagination
1 part inspiration
A shot of sass
A twist of kick ass
Served "up" in a tall pretty glass

I believe most problems can self correct with a new pair of shoes. I love entertaining and being entertained! In my world, black cars rule and anything sparkly is cool. I'm enthusiastic, a bit sarcastic and love a life that's full of F-A-N-T-A-S-T-I-C!

This is more than just a cocktail book. It's a party permit for you to restore your social mojo and get circulating again.

I hope you enjoy some of my road-tested libations and are inspired to share them with your girlfriends.

Enjoy life, wear pretty jewelry and drink amazing cocktails!

Cheers!

KIKI

Open Bar

Bar Basics, Tools, Supplies

Liquid Assets

Setting Up Your Bar

Mise en place: a French culinary term for "everything in place". Having everything prepared and ready when you need it is cardinal rule number one when setting up your very own liquid lounge.

Don't wait until you're having a party to get set up. I can't count how many times a girlfriend has dropped by and I offer her a cocktail only to find out, I don't have the necessary ingredients. I stood in the kitchen frozen in time hoping that the vodka bottle will magically become full again, or, that the ice maker somehow will produce ice at warp speed.

You don't need a lot of variety to set up your bar. At first, just the basics will suffice. Then, as you start getting creative or have a hankering for something outside the norm, you can add to it.

I love to entertain and I'm all about ambiance and details. Whether you're throwing a large cocktail party or just having a few girls over for some chit-chat, nothing gets people in a party mood better than great drinks and an upbeat, unforgettable atmosphere.

With that said, don't forget all the fun little details when setting up your bar. The cute cocktail napkins, swizzle sticks, drink umbrellas, fun straws and, for goddess sake, make sure you create a special playlist on your iPod so when the party's jumpin' your beats are a thumpin'.

Be creative and have fun.

Happy cocktailing!

V . I . S .

Very Important Spirits & Other Essential Ingredients

Naturally, you'll set your bar up with the spirits that you like. However, keep in mind that not all of your guests share the same palette. A well stocked bar always has a variety of spirits, mixers and garnishes.

Throughout this book I may reference a particular brand here and there, but that's just my taste buds talking. I recommend starting with the basics, and as your cocktailing skills elevate, you can start experimenting and acquire your own preferences.

Girlfriend to Girlfriend tip: If you're using a premium spirit, stick with quality ingredients from start to finish. (Great + Great = Divine)

The list below will get you started on building your spirit repertoire.

SPIRITS

Bourbon
Gin
Rum (white)
Tequila

Vermouth (dry white and sweet red)
Vodka (plain)

OPTIONAL SPIRITS

Rum (dark/spiced)
Vodka (flavored)

LIQUEURS:

Grand Marnier (Triple Sec if you're on a budget) or, any other orange flavored liqueur
Velvet Falernum –an addictive blend of ingredients!
St. Germaine Elderflower – (There are less expensive ones, but this is my fave!)

MIXERS

Tonic Water (if you use diet expect a different flavor profile)
Soda Water
Ginger Ale
Cranberry Juice, pineapple juice
Tomato juice (V8)
Cola (diet/regular)

CITRUS (lemon, lime, orange, grapefruit)

Citrus is very important in cocktails and is NOT peeled. In certain cocktails, the oil from the peel can be as important as the juice. Always wash your citrus before using.

Fresh citrus juice adds a delicious layer of flavor to a cocktail that you just can't get from premade juice. Make sure your citrus is at room temperature before using, roll it on the counter before cutting to maximize the juice and always cut your citrus close to when you're going to use it to prevent it from drying out.

Tip: *if you have a stubborn little citrus that doesn't want to juice, simply pop it in the microwave for about 15 seconds.*

HERBS

Herbs bring an aromatic quality to the party! Herbs bring that "wow" factor to a drink. Remember to wash your herbs gently and thoroughly before using them.

For maximum flavor, use the stems as well as the leaves and tear them before dropping them into your shaker.

I like to store my herbs in a small glass filled with a little water. I find that arranging my herbs in a little bouquet is a convenient and efficient use of space in my bar. (Plus, it looks cute!)

My favorite herbs are:

Thyme, basil, mint, rosemary and cilantro

THE BITTER TRUTH!

Bitters come in a myriad of flavors from the classic Angostura, to orange, grapefruit, rhubarb and everything in between. They're essential in certain cocktails and are perfect when you think your cocktail needs a little "something-something" but don't know what. A little goes a long way so start with just a few dashes and go from there.

Girlfriend to Girlfriend tip: bitters add a nice little zing to sparkling water! Remember, just a little dab will do ya!

SIMPLE SYRUP

Simple syrup is a bar staple. When making specialty drinks, this ingredient is as important as the volume button on your stereo! Simple syrup is like a magic potion. When added to a cocktail with a strong flavor profile, it smoothes and balances the other ingredients.

Girlfriend to Girlfriend tip: Infusing herbs, rose petals, spices, citrus and teas into your simple syrup is a cocktail game changer and will basically give you instant rock star status with all your peeps. (More on that later).

Making your own is super simple and lasts up to 3 months if stored in the refrigerator.

Here is the classic recipe:

1 cup water
1 cup sugar

Mix the water and sugar together in a small saucepan. Bring to a boil over medium-high heat. Let boil for about 1 minute and immediately remove from heat.

Cool completely before storing in a clean bottle with lid.

Note: in a pinch you can use agave syrup (a common sweetener in margaritas). Agave syrup can be purchased in most liquor stores.

Bar Essentials
Tools . Glassware . Ice

Just like in cooking, having the right tools makes all the difference. You don't have to spend an arm and a leg, just purchase a few good quality basics and you're good to go.

Here's your shopping list:

Shaker: There are 2 types. (Pick the one you like) The classic, 3-piece shaker comes with the canister, a cap and a lid with a built in strainer. Then there is the Boston-style shaker. It consists of a mixing glass and a stainless-steel canister. It does not come with a strainer, so you will need to purchase one separately.

Girlfriend to Girlfriend tip: I prefer the latter of the shakers and use a Hawthorne strainer. Either one does the job, but on those days you want your cocktail in your glass pronto, pouring it through the little holes on the classic 3-piece strainer feels like watching paint dry.

Hawthorne strainer: a circular strainer with a spring coil around it.

Jigger: I prefer a metal jigger that measures 1 ounce on one end and ½ ounce on the other. (This isn't college anymore. You need a jigger! Until you get your skills down pat, too much or too little makes all the difference in taste)

Muddler: This is your "Louisville Slugger" for cocktails. Looks like a bat and comes in wood or stainless.

Long-handled bar spoon

Channel knife for zesting

Pour spouts: makes for mess free pouring

Small cutting board

GLASSWARE

I love pretty glassware. In fact, I love glassware so much that 9 times out of 10 I'll select my glass first, then, I decide what cocktail gets to step inside.

Keep in mind that most drink recipes are for standard size glassware. You may have to manipulate the recipe a little if you're using a glass that is either too large or too small.

I recommend keeping things simple at first and start with some basic glassware.

Martini Glass (aka, cocktail glass): generally comes in a 4oz – 8oz capacity. The smaller ounce stems work great for Martinis and the larger capacity stems are perfect for "up" cocktails with more ingredients.

Highball Glass: tall and thin, usually holds 8-14 ounces

Rocks Glass: short and wide, usually holds 6-8 ounces

Champagne Flute

Wine Glass

Shot Glass: I prefer tall and uniquely shaped so I can use them for mini desserts, cocktail "flights" and of course, shots!

Girlfriend to Girlfriend tip: Any vessel that is food safe can be used as barware. Mixing new, old, fancy and casual glassware is super fun and is always a good conversation starter. (Hello trip to the flea market!)

ICE

Ice is super important in making cocktails. Always use fresh ice. (Ice that tastes like your freezer isn't good). Using store purchased ice cubes is fine when making drinks served on the rocks, but when making drinks in your shaker you will need to use an ice mallet (or brick covered in plastic wrap) to break them into smaller cubes.

Don't run out! (Total buzz kill when this happens). Rule of thumb is around one pound of ice per person when hosting a party.

Measure-Up

Measurements & Equivalents for Successful Cocktailing

Measurements are very important in cocktailing, and just the slightest variation can make your drink taste completely different.

¼ ounce = 1 ½ teaspoons
½ ounce = 1 tablespoon
1 ounce = 2 tablespoons
1 ½ ounces = 3 tablespoons
2 ounces = 1/4 cup
4 ounces = ½ cup
8 ounces – 1 cup

750 ml bottle = 25.4 ounces (3 cups)
1 liter bottle = 33.8 ounces (approximately 4 ¼ cup)
1 medium lime = approximately 1 ounce
1 medium lemon = approximately 1 ½ ounce
1 medium orange = approximately 2 ½ - 3 ounces

Bar Speak

Terms you should know

Every domestic bartendress needs to establish a little street cred with her home girls. Memorizing some bar lingo will go a long way in building your confidence and upping your game in the cocktail world.

Plus, it will prevent having a cocktail meltdown in the middle of making a drink.

Girlfriend to Girlfriend tip: Don't offer to make a specialty cocktail until you have mastered the art of it. While there are a lot of variations of modern cocktails, classic cocktails like Martinis and Manhattans should be made old school unless specifically requested to be altered.

TERMS

Neat – (This does not mean cool or awesome). Neat is a term used when no ice is wanted.

Up – A term used when a drink is served with no ice (usually) in a martini glass

Rocks – A drink is served over ice

Twist – Generally, used when garnishing a martini or a fancy cocktail served up. A twist is a strand of citrus that is peeled (directly over the cocktail), curled and either floats on top or rides along the side of the glass.

Dirty – (Get your mind out of the gutter!) This is martini speak. Dirty means with olive juice.

Shaken – The drink is built in a shaker filled with ice.

Stirred – The drink is stirred with a long spoon and not shaken. This maintains the integrity of certain drinks.

Champagne Float – A term used when the cocktail is made and poured into its serving glass then finished with just a splash, or "float" of champagne on top.

Back or chaser – This is NOT when you chase the drinkee around the bar, nor is it when you turn your back on them. When someone requests a back or a chaser, they are asking for an additional drink to finish with. Most common are a beer back, after a shot of alcohol, or, a water back, after a stiff drink or shot.

Rinse – A rinse is when a small amount of a spirit or liqueur is swirled around inside the glass, then dumped out before pouring in the cocktail. Doing this adds another layer of flavor in a subtle way.

Call Drink – This is *not* bitching out your drink or calling it names just because you had a bad day. This refers to the type of alcohol you request that your drink be made with.

Mocktail – A non-alcoholic drink. *(Why bother! It's like drinking decaffeinated coffee).* Unless, you're the designated driver! Then I think it's totally awesome.

Let's Get This Party Started!

I love getting ready to go out for the night. It's a lot like theatre. Theatre has "acts" that lead up to the main event, and, for me, getting ready is a series of acts in itself.

In Act one, I read the script. By this I mean accessing the scene. Where am I going? What's the vibe? What's the dress code? Then, I set the stage. Act Two is the preparation, Act Three gets me in the mood and Act Four is when the curtain goes up, or, when the door bell rings and your guests have arrived to pick you up and head out the door for the night.

In this chapter, you'll find cocktails (and music) that will definitely get you in the party mood before hitting the door! (Not too much, just a little primer).

I think the "pre-funk" that takes place at home beforehand is almost as fun as the main event. For me the pre-funk starts early. I start by creating a home-spa atmosphere in my bathroom. Candles, music, mask and bath. That whole ritual is followed up with a quick change in music and a trip to the "liquid lounge", aka the kitchen, to craft the perfect cocktail and kick things up a notch.

A little mix, muddle and shake and with drink in tow, I'm off to my dressing room (aka, bedroom) to gaze into my closet and see what outfit gets to go out for the night.

Usually, I get hung up on the outfit thing and move right into shoes and jewelry. After a few trial dance moves to see how the shoes are going to perform, it's off to the bathroom again to lock down my curls, apply make-up and dab a touch of perfume on.

At this point one of two things happens. One, I get "re-dressed" because of a wardrobe malfunction or just simply changed my mind. Two, I make another cocktail to buy me some more time while I figure out what the heck to wear!

Have fun tonight and drink responsibly!

Girls Night

Sips while you primp

The Cat Walk

(Think of this as a Shirley Temple all grown up!)

A true girlie girl drink! You're fresh out of the shower, already applied shimmer cream to your skin and you're ready to party.

I can't remember where I was when I read this, but I loved it! It read "if your glass is half empty, drink faster. If your glass *IS* empty, order another. (fō shō!)

Playlist: "Pour Some Sugar on Me" – Def Leopard

Supplies: pretty rocks glass & shaker

Ingredients

2 ounces Seagram's 7
3 ounces 7-up
Lime wedge
Grenadine

Fill cocktail shaker with ice, squeeze lime wedge and drop into shaker. Add Seagram's 7 and 7-Up. Stir vigorously and pour into a rocks glass. "Float" a little grenadine on top, garnish with a long stem cherry and enjoy.

Girlfriend to Girlfriend tip: For some reason, wearing the perfect shade of red lipstick gives this drink that "oh no you didn't" taste!

The Stiletto

You just got a text message from your BFF telling you she'll be over at 8:00 o'clock to pick you up. You're not sure what to wear, but you do know you're going to wear the hottest shoes in your closet.

Take it from me, bust a few quick dance moves just to make certain you and the shoes are on the same page. There's nothing sexy about a pretty girl holding her shoes on the dance floor while her feet are getting black and sticky!

Playlist: "Glamorous" – Fergie (featuring Ludacris)

Supplies: martini glass, shaker and plenty of attitude

Ingredients

3 ounces premium vodka
1 ounce Lillet Blanc *(French brand of aperitif)*
2 fresh strawberries
Lemon twist

Fill shaker with cracked ice. Build your cocktail by first dropping the strawberries into the shaker and muddle. Combine liquid ingredients and shake well. Strain into a chilled martini glass and garnish with a lemon twist.

Girlfriend to Girlfriend tip: For maximum shoe envy tonight make sure your kicks are polished and in tip top shape. Nothing looks worse than scuffed toes and the nail popping out of your heel!

Bonus tip: High fives to my frugal fashionistas, but, if your shoes came from the sale rack, please completely remove the price sticker on your soles! (This screams major blue light shopper).

Bombshell

You're having a good hair day, you just applied falsies to the outer corner of your lashes, and basically, you're ready to kick ass and take names.

This is no time for rush decisions in the closet. Try a couple different outfits on, do a few "drive-by's in the mirror", and confirm what you already know (that you look ah-ah-ahhhhmazing).

Now, make tracks to the kitchen and whip up a glass of liquid courage.

Playlist: "Single Ladies" – Beyoncé

Supplies: pretty rocks glass, shaker *(sexy chandelier earrings optional)*

Ingredients

3 ounces gin
½ ounce simple syrup
3 fresh raspberries
2 fresh basil leaves

Fill shaker with ice, drop raspberries and basil in shaker and muddle. Add Gin and simple syrup. Shake it like ya' mean it and strain into an ice filled glass.

Girlfriend to Girlfriend tip: You know you've picked the right outfit if you look in the mirror and say "oh yeah, I'd date me".

Old School

We all have nights that the thought of getting all gussied up to go out sounds like more trouble than it's worth. On those nights, I invite some friends over for a little girl's night in. Who am I kidding; it's an excuse for me to get my inner DJ on. Back in the day, I completely tore up my Run DMC record (and my turntable) home schooling myself on the art of "scratching". These days, I just hit shuffle and let my iPod do the work!

Playlist: Anything from Run DMC, Sugar Hill Gang or Beastie Boys will have you on your feet in no time.

Supplies: Tall cocktail glasses, shaker

(Sporting a pair of Beats by Dr. Dre headphones around your neck is the perfect accessory for the night!)

Ingredients

2 ounces light rum
1 ounce simple syrup
Juice from ½ lime
6 fresh blueberries
3 sprigs of mint
Club soda

Combine blueberries, mint sprigs and simple syrup in shaker. Muddle until well combined. Fill with ice, add rum and shake. Pour into a tall ice filled glass and top with club soda. Put the drinks on a pretty tray and strut out of the kitchen like you're on a catwalk!

Girlfriend to Girlfriend tip: Be warned sisters, these babies go down easy. You're going to need some carbs tonight so plan ahead. (This is no night for a hummus and veggie platter). Put your pizza man on speed dial, or, if you have an iphone, have "Siri" give him a call around Ten o'clock.

Fishnet Stocking

Tonight you decide that your "go to" accessory of the night will be your fishnet stockings. You go with your bad self!

Playlist: "She's Got Legs"- ZZ Top

Supplies: Martini glass, shaker, black rimming sugar*

*(black sugar can be found at most specialty baking stores)

Ingredients

3 ounces Jack Daniels
3 ounces diet cola
½ ounce grenadine
Cherry for garnish

Combine all ingredients in shaker filled with ice, stir with a long spoon and strain into a well chilled martini glass rimmed with black sugar. Garnish with a stemmed cherry. (I see a catwalk in your future)

Note: sprinkle the black rimming sugar on a saucer. Run a lime wheel around the rim of your glass and press firmly against the saucer.

Girlfriend to Girlfriend tip: To spare your toes from looking like little smokies popping through your fishnets, (NOT sexy) put a thin pair of socks on *before* your fishnets. Thank me later!

Hot Mess

We all have at least one girlfriend that's super fun to go out with until she's had too many, right?   Totally lame flirting gestures, stumbling all over the place, baby talk and clothes that start to come off. There's really no other name for her, other than a HOT MESS.

Playlist: "Born This Way" – Lady Gaga

Supplies: Martini Glass, Shaker, super fine rimming sugar

Ingredients

1 ounce Yatzi ginger vodka
1 ounce Cucumber Vodka
1 ounce fresh lemon juice
1 ounce simple syrup
Small slice Jalapeno Pepper (no seeds)
Thin slice fresh cucumber

Fill cocktail shaker with ice, drop in the fresh cucumber and jalapeno slices and muddle. Add remaining ingredients, shake well, strain and pour into a sugar rimmed martini glass. (Check your pulse after this one!)

Girlfriend to Girlfriend tip: If someone you know starts entering the hot mess zone please do not take her to a Karaoke bar, let her call her ex-boyfriend, tweet or FB post. And god forbid, absolutely no uploading pictures in real time. *(Remember, there is no cyber delete key)*

Bitch-Slap

I can't be the only one that has dreamed of putting an out of hand girlfriend in check! (I've never actually done this, but certainly the thought has crossed my mind). I've had girlfriends pissed at me because I had a boyfriend and they didn't. I've had girlfriends drink the "hate-r-aide" because I lost a few pounds and they didn't. I've watched girlfriends act like a total ding dong in front of a guy trying to get noticed.

It's those moments I wanted to *"bitch-slap"* you girlfriend, but instead I just said "pull up your big girl thong and join the party".

Playlist: "Mama Said Knock You Out" – LL Cool J

Supplies: Shaker, martini glass, and boxing gloves

Ingredients

2 ounces gold rum
1 ounce mango nectar
1 ounce guava nectar
1 small wedge fresh lime
1 pineapple chunk

In a shaker filled with ice squeeze lime wedge and drop in. Add fresh pineapple chunk and muddle. Add remaining ingredients and shake your aggravations out. Strain and pour into a well chilled martini glass.

Singapore
Fizz-izzle

Before you decide to go on an unsocial hiatus tonight, make one of these babies and I bet half way through you'll be ready to party!

Playlist: "Pump Up the Jam" – Salt N Pepa

Supplies: Cute cocktail glass

Ingredients

1 ounce fresh lemon juice
½ ounce simple syrup
1 ounce cherry brandy
1 ¼ ounce gin
Splash of soda water

Combine all ingredients except the soda water in a shaker filled with ice. Shake and pour directly into a well chilled cocktail glass. Finish with a splash of soda water on top. Garnish with a cherry.

Chapter 2

This chapter is all about love potions in a cup. Next time you're feeling giddy about your man or someone you're crushing on, mix up a pair of these delicious intoxicating cocktails and ignite the fire.

But remember, guys are wired differently than us. Just because you had one or two awesome dates, doesn't mean he's all in!

Proceed with caution. Crawl before your walk. Enjoy the moment and see where it ends up.

In the meantime, enjoy one of the cocktails I've created for you.

Best wishes and plenty of kisses!

Love Potions

Cloud 9

Still dreamy over the guy you had dinner with last night? Pay homage to him by making this drink and pondering "what if?"

Playlist: "Call Me Maybe" – Carly Rae Jepsen

Supplies: Martini glass, shaker, whipped cream, edible gold glitter

Ingredients

2 ounces Bombay Sapphire gin
1 ounce fresh lemon juice
1 ounce peach schnapps
1/4 ounce simple syrup
2 ounces fresh orange juice
Whipped cream garnish (you gotta' make a little cloud!)

Combine all ingredients except the whipped cream in a shaker filled with ice, shake, strain and pour into a well chilled martini glass. Float a dollop of fresh whipped cream in the center, sprinkle with glitter and let the dreaming begin!

Girlfriend to Girlfriend tip: I get that you're totally excited right now, but please do not call him and talk all cutsie-ish. Just enjoy your cocktail and chill out.

He's The One

Once in our lives someone comes along and knocks us off our high heels!

In this case, it happened to yours truly! Six lovely years ago I met my husband at an event. The moment I saw him smile I thought, WOW, I'm intrigued. I love people that smile a lot. Especially, for no reason at all.

Fast forward 5 days, and we couldn't get enough of each other. I feel like I should write a thank you note to Bombay Sapphire! I'll tell you what, if you want some no frills conversation, where you call a spade a spade, this is all you. (We've since named this drink "The Truth").

Two weeks later we're off to the beach and on the way, he pops in a Santana CD and said "listen to the words". Right back atchya' baby.

Playlist: "You and I" – Carlos Santana (supernatural album)

Supplies: Cocktail glass and a great guy to drink it with

Ingredients

3 ounces Bombay Sapphire gin
Served on the rocks with a lemon twist!

Change of Heart

We've all heard the old adage, "you don't know you're happy until you're happy". And it's true.

I would consider myself pretty lucky as far as relationships go. In my dating years I was never a serial dater. I pretty much dated only a handful or so quality guys over the years, most of which I would consider some of my best friends even now. A lot of people think that's weird, but I say if you get out *before* things get dicey, you still have a cool friendship intact!

I've had relationships that I thought were fun, and that I *thought* I was happy in, but once I met my husband, I realized what happy really felt like. I remember him saying to me early on when we were dating "we just seem to fit". I would have to say that is the *purrrrrfect* way to describe it.

Playlist: "Postcard from Paris" – The Band Perry

Supplies: Mixing glass, short cocktail glass, cute straw

Ingredients

2 ounces vodka
½ ounce crème de coconut
½ ounce peach schnapps
3 ounces fresh squeezed orange juice
Float of grenadine

Fill a bar glass half way with ice. Pour in all ingredients except the grenadine. Stir a few times with a bar spoon and strain into an ice filled cocktail glass. Float a little grenadine on the top (don't mix in) and serve with a cute straw. (Tastes delicious with a heart shaped sugar cookie)

Girlfriend to Girlfriend tip: Sit down in your comfy chair, grab your ipad and plan a trip to Paris. Even if it's just a virtual trip, you'll still have fun researching. Bon Voyage!

French Kiss

Mon Chéri! You're simply giddy right now over the thought of him. This oughta calm you down and put a devilish smile on your beautiful face.

Playlist: "Kiss" - Prince

Supplies: Eiffel tower champagne glass (**www.Zgallerie.com**) or any other pretty champagne glass. Pink rose petal for garnish

Ingredients

½ ounce crème de violette
Champagne (Proseco)

Pour crème de violette in the bottom of a champagne glass. Fill with champagne and finish by floating a rose petal on top. (You're going to think you died and, well, went to France).

Girlfriend to Girlfriend tip: Drinking this cocktail while nibbling on a petit four with a stack of European design magazines at your side is a delicious way to spend the afternoon. Mahwah!

The Seducer

Slow down little temptress. Don't give the milk away for free! Make him work for it.

Playlist: "Lets' get it on" – Marvin Gaye

Supplies: Martini glass, shaker, zester

Ingredients

2 ounces premium vodka
1 ounce Limoncello
1/2 ounce simple syrup
Sprig of fresh rosemary
Lemon twist

Fill shaker with ice, add 1 sprig of fresh rosemary and muddle. Leave sprig in shaker, add vodka, Limoncello and simple syrup. Shake vigorously, strain and pour into a well chilled martini glass. Garnish with a small piece of rosemary and a lemon twist. (Can I get a "hell yeah"?)

Girlfriend to girlfriend tip: A fresh manicure, pretty pink lip gloss and a fun little statement ring on your index finger is the perfect accompaniment to this well deserved cocktail!

Sugar Daddy

I have a friend that swears by millionairematch.com to help find financial bliss. I'm no Suzie Orman, but for shit sake, just because he "says" he's a millionaire doesn't mean he is. (Too bad your membership doesn't come with a .pdf of his 1040's!). *Just sayin'*

A few years ago I was at a girlfriend's birthday party and spent most of the night talking to her grandmother who had been recently widowed. I asked her if she would ever remarry. With no hesitation she said "sweetheart, at my age men are either looking for a purse or a nurse". I laughed my ass off!

Playlist: "Billionaire" – Bruno Mars

Supplies: Martini glass, shaker, fresh mint leaves

Ingredients

2 ounces premium tequila
1/2 ounce NAVAN pure vanilla liqueur
1 ounce Cointreau
1 ounce fresh lime juice
Mint leaves for garnish

Combine all ingredients in a shaker filled with ice, shake, strain and pour into a martini glass. Garnish with mint leaf.

Strip Tease

A long time ago I was in this bar and a guy walked up to me and said "nice dress, it would look better on *my* floor". P-leeeze!

If you're looking to kick things up a notch, this is all you sister.

Playlist: "Walk This Way" – Aerosmith

Ingredients

2 ounces Jägermeister
1 ounce of dark rum

(Told you I wasn't kidding)

The Pole Dancer

Clearly you're not afraid, and for that I raise my glass to you girl-friend. With that said, I triple dog dare you to drink more than one of these babies. Bottoms' up!

A long time ago I personally nicknamed this drink the break-up/make-up drink. I made this cocktail the night my ex-boyfriend and I broke-up. By the time we were finished we forgot that we were broken up and dated for another few months!

Playlist: "Private Dancer" – Tina Turner

Supplies: short cocktail glass, silver metallic straw (because it looks like a "pole" silly!)

Ingredients

2 ounces Hpnotiq Liqueur
2 ounces citrus vodka
Club soda
Lemon wheel for garnish

Pour Hpnotiq and vodka in an ice-filled glass. Top with club soda and garnish with lemon wheel. (Boom shakalaka)

Girlfriend to Girlfriend tip: You've officially been warned my pretties. If there was a cocktail that should come with a warning label, this would be it.

Chapter 3

This chapter goes out to all of my girlfriends (that includes you if your reading this book) that have been through love hell and back.

Whether you're the "leavee" or the "leaveor", it's not great. Nobody likes a liar-liar pants on fire! Being lied to or cheated on, (basically same dif) sucks.

Listening to my girlfriends, co-workers and even perfect strangers discuss their woe's over the years, I've come to the realization that the one common thread we all share is there is no "WHY".

We all ask it, but any possible explanation to this little 3 letter word, is THERE IS NO EXPLANATION!

So if life presents you with the question of why again, take a deep breath, sit back, fasten your seatbelt and make one of the delicious cocktails in this chapter.

A few sips of these bad boys and you won't even remember who or why you're supposed to be pissed at.

Cheers!

K.M.A!
(Kiss my ass)
Break-up Drinking

Whoop Ass in a Glass

I think we've all wanted to open a can at some point in our dating or married lives right? Well, if that's how you're feeling right now, then I've got you covered with this one.

Playlist: "f*** You" – by Cee Lo Green

Supplies: rocks glass and matches

Ingredients

3 ounces premium tequila
½ ounce grenadine
Fresca soda
Slice of fresh grapefruit

Pour tequila in an ice-filled glass. Fill glass with Fresca soda and float the grenadine on top. Garnish with a slice of fresh grapefruit.

Girlfriend to Girlfriend tip: Don't spend any more of your precious energy stewing over him! Your final hurrah is after drinking this cocktail, use the matches to burn his picture. Poof! All gone...

"Go with the guy that messes up your lipstick, not your mascara"

unknown

The Flip-Tini

Sometimes it's hard to refrain from using our "third man", "middle digit", "Mr. Tall Man", "the bird" or whatever else you want to call it. Fact is our middle finger is a silent but effective tool we can use to communicate.

Note: This drink tastes a whole lot better if you raise your middle finger while sipping.

Playlist: "You Give Love A Bad Name" – Bon Jovi

Supplies: Shaker, martini glass*

Optional: Giant cocktail ring to wear on your "flipping" finger. It makes it a little more ladylike.

Ingredients

2 ounces premium vodka
1 ounce Grand Marnier
1 ounce cranberry juice
1 ounce fresh lemon juice
Lemon twist for garnish

Combine all ingredients in shaker filled with ice, shake, strain and pour into a well chilled martini glass. Garnish with the lemon twist.

Sip, Flip and Feel better!

The Decision Maker

Not feeling the love and don't know what to do? You will after this drink.

Playlist: "50 Ways to Leave Your Lover" – Paul Simon

Supplies: Brandy glass, heat proof low ball glass, hot water and a note pad to make a list of pros and cons of the relationship.

(This is where visual clarity comes in)

Ingredients

2 ounces premium brandy
1/2 ounce Navan vanilla liqueur

Combine both ingredients in a brandy glass. Heat over the low ball glass filled with hot water. (Hold on to your bar stool sisters! Smooth, but potent).

The Cheater

Look, you're never going to figure it out so don't even try. Here's the math: Cheat + Cheat = Kiss My Ass.

Good news. This recipe calls for 2 drinks. (Yippee!) One is for you and one is for "her"---she can have him.

Playlist: "Before He Cheats" – Carrie Underwood

Supplies: 2 shot glasses, salt for rimming *your** glass, lime wedge

Ingredients

Drink #1 (represents YOU)

1 shot extra cold top shelf tequila
*Pour into a salt rimmed shot glass, bite into the lime and shoot

Drink #2 (represents HER)

1 shot extra cold top shelf tequila
*no more salt (your blood pressure is high enough) – just drink!

Note: After drinking delete his number from your phone

Girlfriend to Girlfriend tip: Remember the game "knock knock"? Well, if you need extra help getting over him call your girlfriend and ask her to play it with yez!

Her: Knock-Knock?
You: Who's there?
Her: {she'll insert the cheaters name here}
You: {cheaters name} who?
Her: Exactly! Done

Son of a Beach

Breaking up can be bittersweet. We've all been through it. First you can't imagine life without the guy, then, you're just plain-ole mad, and finally, you hit the red zone, or the "oh no he didn't" zone and you're done.

Once you're in "the zone" you can actually see it for what it is. Let's face it, rarely do people break up for no reason right? With that said, focus your energy on the future and give the past a swift kick in the pants and move on.

Here's to a fresh start!

Playlist: "Hit the Road Jack" - Ray Charles

Supplies: Cute cocktail glass, shaker, cocktail umbrella and your favorite travel magazine. (It's time to pack your bags and go somewhere tropical)

Ingredients

2 ounces Malibu Rum
1 ounce vodka
½ ounce Maraschino liqueur
Diet Coke
Pineapple wedge for garnish

Combine everything except Diet Coke in a shaker filled with ice. Shake out all your anger and strain into the cocktail glass. Top with Diet Coke and garnish with the pineapple wedge.

Girlfriend to Girlfriend tip: Immediately following this drink, book a spa day including an eyebrow wax then start planning your vacation.

Have fun in the sun!

Love shackle

This drink goes out to all the ladies that had the strength to grab the key, unlock the love shackle and move on. Breaking up doesn't have to be full of drama and tears. Breaking up just means both of you had the cahonas to admit its not working. So, eat a little humble pie on the way out the door, learn from *your* shortcomings and get your game face on for the next lucky guy.

There's someone out there for everyone. Don't settle!

Playlist: "Just Fine" – Mary J Blige

Supplies: Cocktail shaker, pretty martini glass and a new party dress

Ingredients

2 ounces Absolut pear vodka
1 ounce plain vodka
3 ounces Seagram's ginger ale
1 sprig fresh thyme
Lemon twist

In a shaker filled with ice drop in the fresh thyme and muddle gently. Add pear vodka and plain vodka. Shake until cold and strain into a chilled martini glass. Top with ginger ale and garnish with the lemon twist.

Designated Driver Drinks & The Morning after Remedies

Driving While Sober (D.W.S.)

It's only fair we take our turn at the wheel. Actually, it's not all bad, you feel better in the morning, there's no risk of having beer goggles and you don't have to wonder if you texted anyone you shouldn't have.

Playlist: "You Ain't Much Fun Since I Quit Drinkin" – Toby Keith

Supplies: Tall cocktail glass

Ingredients

½ cup lemon sparkling mineral water
 4 Fresh Mint leaves
¼ cup fresh or frozen blackberry's (pureed)
Teaspoon of sugar
Lemon wheel for garnish

Fill tall glass ½ up with ice. Add mint sprigs and sugar. Gently muddle. Add blackberry puree and mineral water. Stir vigorously. Fill the rest of the glass up with ice and garnish with a lemon wheel.

No Screw, Just the Driver

Just because you're going sans alcohol tonight doesn't mean you can't have a delicious drink. This is a take on the classic screwdriver. It's delicious, full of vitamin C and unlike its alcohol fueled counterpart; it won't ruin your day tomorrow!

Playlist: "Raise Your Glass" – P!nk

Supplies: Shaker, tall cocktail glass, juicer

Ingredients

Juice of ½ a blood orange
Juice of ½ a lime
2 ounces of pineapple juice
1 ounce coco loco (found in most supermarkets, liquor stores)
1 ounce cranberry juice
Soda water

Combine all ingredients in shaker filled with ice, shake, strain & pour into a tall ice filled glass. Finish by floating a little soda water on top. Enjoy!

Girlfriend to Girlfriend tip: This drink tastes way better when wearing a wrist full of amazing bracelets on your drinking arm.

You go girl!

Mockarita

Meet Mockarita, Margarita's virgin sister. This cocktail is so delicious; the only thing you'll miss is a headache in the morning.

Have fun tonight Senorita!

Play list: "Macarena" – Los Del Rio

Supplies: Shaker, tall glass

Ingredients

3 ounces limeade
Juice from ¼ medium orange
5-6 leaves of fresh cilantro
Lime flavored sparkling water
Lime wedge for garnish

Fill shaker with ice. Drop in cilantro leaves and muddle. Add limeade, juice from orange wedge and shake well. Strain into ice filled glass. Top with lime flavored sparkling water and garnish with the lime wedge.

Clear Headed

This drink is just the ticket after a good workout or during a home spa treatment following last night's train wreck.

Playlist: "The Lazy Song" – Bruno Mars

Supplies: Tall glass and perhaps a couple cucumber slices for your eyes!

Ingredients

1 cup water (still or sparkling)
1 sprig fresh cilantro
1 sprig fresh mint
Small slice fresh ginger
2 lemon slices (thin)
1 slice orange
2 lime slices (thin)

In a tall glass, arrange all ingredients and let stand for 15 minutes at room temperature. Before drinking, fill the glass with ice, stir and sip.

Girlfriend to Girlfriend tip: Take advantage of your lazy day by getting a few of those mindless tasks done that you've been putting off. (*Like...*cleaning out your purse or make-up drawer)

The Hangover

I get it. It's one of those mornings that you woke up with last night's make-up on and swear you're not drinking for at least a month. (Yeah, whatever) So you got your swerve on a little too much last night and unfortunately, time is your only friend right now. Before you resort to a little *hair of the pooch*, try this concoction instead. I swear it will have you on your feet in a few hours.

Playlist: "Blame It on the Alcohol" – Jamie Foxx

Supplies: Shaker, tall glass, Aspirin

Ingredients

1 cup tomato juice
½ tsp lemon zest
½ ounce fresh lemon juice
Dash of Worcestershire sauce
¼ tsp fresh prepared horseradish
Celery salt to taste
Fresh ground pepper to taste
Long stock of fresh crisp celery

Combine all ingredients in a shaker filled with ice. Shake until you break a sweat, and strain into a tall, ice filled glass. Garnish with a celery stalk.

Girlfriend to Girlfriend tip: Give yourself a couple hours then go for a brisk walk. Once your blood starts pumping you still have a shot at getting a few things done today. Whatever you do, don't opt for the greasy pizza or burger thing. It's a gut bomb and will not make you feel any better.

REHAB-ulous

Ok, those nights need to come to a screeching halt my sister. Are you kidding me right now? Hopefully there's no collateral damage from last nights' throw back from your college days.

It's time to get those electrolytes fired back up. Drink this and for god sake, pinky swear you won't have a night like that again.

Playlist: "Rehab" – Amy Winehouse

Supplies: Tall glass

Ingredients

¾ cup Orange Gatorade (or your favorite sports drink)
Lime slice
Orange slice
Fresh Tarragon sprig
2 ounces Soda water

Fill tall glass half way with ice. Add the Gatorade, lime slice, orange slice and tarragon sprig. Stir. Fill the glass with more ice and top with a little soda water.

Girlfriend to Girlfriend tip: Once you're feeling a little better, call your girlfriends and make sure there aren't any fires you need to put out from last night's circus. If there is, immediately put your crisis management hat on and go to work.

Liquid Dessert

Vanilla Ice

Anything vanilla puts me in a great mood. This drink makes me want to get in my PJ's, put my hair up, rent Easy A (if you haven't seen it, it's funnier than hell) and sip on this while you laugh until your sides hurt!

Playlist: wait for it----"Ice Ice Baby" – Vanilla Ice

(Yeah, I went there)

Supplies: Martini shaker, vanilla wafers, martini glass (fuzzy slippers optional)

Ingredients

Crushed vanilla wafers for rimming
Orange wedge (for rimming)

1 1/2 ounce vanilla vodka
1 1/2 ounce Kahlua
3 ounces 1% milk

Run the orange wedge around a martini glass. Dip the rim of the glass in a plate with crushed vanilla wafers. Next, combine all ingredients in an ice filled shaker, shake, strain, and pour into a martini glass.

(Holla! You might want to save at least one wafer to nosh on while sipping)

Float 21

(Because you need to be 21 to drink it)

This drink is for those of us who prefer to skip the dessert tray and sip our dessert instead.

Playlist: "Bringin' Sexy Back" – Justin Timberlake

Supplies: Tall glass, cute straw, long spoon

Ingredients

1 ounce Godiva chocolate vodka
1 ounce Godiva raspberry vodka
1 ounce Starbucks coffee liqueur
¼ cup Soda water
Small scoop of vanilla bean ice cream
*Whipped cream (for topping) *optional
Mint leaf garnish
Fresh raspberry garnish

Combine first 3 ingredients in a tall glass filled half way up with ice. Stir. Add soda water and more ice leaving about 3 inches from the top of the glass. Add ice cream scoop and give it a quick stir.

Add a quick shot of whipped cream. Garnish with a mint leaf and a fresh raspberry.

Super yum!

Hot Cha-Cha

Change my name and call me Maria! This is not your grandmothers hot cocoa. One sip and you'll be saying "Uno more por favor"!

Play list: "Shake Senora" - Pit Bull

Supplies: Tiny size coffee mug and marshmallows.

* Sombrero and Mariachi's optional

Cha-Cha Mix

¾ cup unsweetened cocoa powder
1 ½ tsp ground cinnamon
1 ¼ cup baker's sugar
½ tsp chipotle chile powder
½ tsp ground coriander
¼ tsp nutmeg
¼ cup brown sugar
1 tsp vanilla extract

Mix all ingredients in a bowl until well combined. Will hold at room temperature for 1 ½ months if stored in a glass container with airtight lid.

The Drink

¾ cup hot milk
2 3/4 Tbsp cha-cha mix
3/4 ounce amaretto
1 ounce brandy
Large marshmallow
Cinnamon

Stir cha-cha mix into hot milk until well dissolved. Add amaretto and brandy and stir. Pour into mini mugs and garnish with a marshmallow and a sprinkle of cinnamon.

Chocolate Dipped Strawberry

Seriously, this is the best dessert drink ever! It's fun, whimsical and delicious.

Playlist: "Last Friday Night" – Katy Perry

Supplies: Shaker, martini glass, fresh strawberry puree, fresh mint leaves

Ingredients

Chocolate syrup (like Hershey's)

1 ounce vodka
1 ounce Godiva chocolate vodka
1 ounce whip cream flavored vodka
2 ounces strawberry puree
Fresh strawberry & mint leaf (garnish)

Prepare your glass: Lightly drizzle chocolate syrup directly on the bottom and around the sides of the martini glass.

Combine vodkas & strawberry puree in an ice filled shaker, shake, strain and pour into your prepared glass.

Garnish with a floating mint leaf and a fresh strawberry on the rim of the glass.

Orange Chocolate Martini

This is the perfect love fest of orange and chocolate. It's great for that after dinner sweet tooth, when you're too full for cake!

Playlist: Anything Jack Johnson is great after dinner music

Supplies: Shaker, martini glass

Ingredients

1 ounces vodka
1 ounce chocolate liqueur
¾ ounce Cointreau
Orange twist for garnish

Fill shaker with ice. Add remaining ingredients, shake well and strain into a chilled martini glass. Garnish with an orange twist.

Copa-Ca-Banana

Move over bananas foster! I absolutely love table side bananas foster at a white table cloth restaurant that knows how to fix it. *Ooh la la,* I can smell the butter and sugar melting now.

Well, next time you want to surprise your guests, serve a little table side Copa-Ca-Banana in their glass with a smidgen of homemade banana bread and your guest may never leave!

Until then, make one for yourself and enjoy.

Playlist: "Copacabana" – Barry Manilow

Supplies: Shaker, cute martini glass and a beautiful plate of banana bread

Ingredients

2 ounces Vodka
1 ounce Banana liqueur
1 ounce half and half
Nutmeg

Fill shaker with ice. Add vodka, banana liqueur and half and half. Shake until cold. Strain into a well chilled martini glass. Sprinkle a small amount of grated nutmeg on top just before serving.

Enjoy with a piece of homemade banana bread!

Haute Rocks
Fashionable drinks over ice

Haute Rocks

My book wouldn't be complete without a chapter on fashion in-spired cocktails!

I love reading about fashion and design. I'm inspired by the stories of a fashion designer. Their roots, what inspired them and the empires they have built over time.

Those that know me know that I have been accessorizing practically since birth. Well actually, that isn't too far from the truth since I was donned with my first bracelet while in the hospital. I still have the cute little blue beaded bracelet with white alphabet beads that spell out my name.

Surprisingly, I didn't get my ears pierced until I was 15. My first "real" bling was given to me by my parents on my 13th birthday. It was a 14 karat gold and Amethyst (my birthstone) ring. I still remember opening the package and finding a little velvet box inside.

It's no wonder that my passion for jewelry first lead me to making jewelry as a hobby, then as a nice little side business and finally as an entrepreneur, owning my own boutique for 15 years.

From my cocktail style house to yours, gather up a big stack of fashion magazines, invite some friends over tonight and sample a few of my road tested couture cocktails.

Cheers.

The Coco

Gabrielle "Coco" Chanel was the inspiration behind this drink. We have her to thank for the little black dress, her signature quilted hand bags and the iconic Chanel suit.

I remember when I was young I wanted something "Chanel" so bad that I asked to buy a strand of ribbon that was being used to gift wrap perfume during the holidays at a department store.

The woman was so nice! She not only gave me a long piece of that ribbon, she gave me a Chanel note pad as well. Believe it or not, I still have the ribbon and could never bring myself to write on that special notepad.

Playlist: "Unforgettable" – Nat King Cole

Supplies: Beautiful short cocktail glass

red lipstick and lots of pearl and chain necklaces optional

Ingredients

2 ounces premium vodka
1 ounce St. Germaine Elderflower liqueur
5 ounces club soda
1 lemon wedge

Fill cocktail glass with ice. Pour in vodka, St. Germaine Elderflower liqueur and top with club soda. Squeeze the juice from the lemon wedge and drop in. Give a couple quick stirs with a bar spoon and enjoy!

"I think men with an earring are better prepared for marriage. They've experienced pain and bought jewelry!"

-Unknown

Kitten Heel

Meow! Kitten Heels are the sexy little shoes from the 1950's. The iconic Audrey Hepburn fancied them, almost every woman on Mad Men wears them, and though they're no substitute for the stiletto, that cute curvy heel and oh so perfect heel height most definitely make them a closet staple.

Next time you're out on the prowl, do it in a pair of kitten heels!

Playlist: "Don't Cha" – The Pussycat Dolls

Supplies: short cocktail glass

Girlfriend to Girlfriend tip: Sipping while wearing a pencil skirt, fitted blouse and kitten heels pretty much guarantees total hotness! Add oversized dark sunglasses and be prepared to sign autographs.

Ingredients

1 ½ ounces Maker's Mark Bourbon
½ ounce Solerno blood orange liqueur
½ ounce Aperol aperitivo liqueur
¼ ounce lavender simple syrup*
½ ounce fresh lemon juice
Orange twist

*see sexy simple syrup chapter for recipe

Fill cocktail glass with ice. Add remaining ingredients, stir with a bar spoon and garnish with an orange twist.

45.52

Respectfully named after the legendary blue hope diamond! (All 45.52 carats of it). This beauty has quite a story to tell.

It now resides at the Smithsonian's National Museum of Natural History in Washington D.C. after being donated by Harry Winston. It was said to be his "gift to the world".

I'll drink to that!

Playlist: "Diamonds Are a Girl's Best Friend" – Marilyn Monroe

Supplies: Martini glass and plenty of bling

Ingredients

3 ounces Bombay Sapphire gin
1 ounce grapefruit juice (not ruby red)
1 ounce Maraschino liqueur
Mint sprig

Fill shaker with ice. Add remaining ingredients except mint sprig. Stir gently (Do not shake) and strain into a well chilled martini glass. Garnish with mint sprig.

"The only time I ever said no to a drink was when I misunderstood the question" – *Will Sinclair*

Choo Choo

I personally do not own a pair of Mr. Jimmy Choo's sky high, $2.495.00 suede pumps with Swarovski crystal detailing, but I'd like to.

I'm obsessed with this luxury shoe designer. Unfortunately, if I plan on staying married, shelling out that kind of coin on some kicks would definitely NOT be in my best interest.

However, if any of you reading this are friends, relatives, or not so distant cousin of my idol, put in a good word for me. (Size 9)

In the meantime, enjoy this elegant pairing of spirit and fashion.

Playlist: "Bootylicious" – Destiny's Child

Supplies: Short cocktail glass, attitude

Ingredients

2 ounces premium tequila
½ ounce Cointreau
½ ounce Chambord liqueur (raspberry flavored liqueur)
3 ounces good margarita mix

Fill glass with ice and add remaining ingredients. Stir gently and garnish with a lime twist.

The Tiffany

What girl hasn't dreamed of receiving a gift in that little blue box? I remember the first time I set foot in Tiffany's. It was in San Francisco. I'll never forget walking through those stately steel front doors and their dazzling window displays that lure you in.

The store's laid out into sections. You enter through the "dream" showroom full of luxurious diamonds and gem stones and then it's straight back to what I refer to as the "semi affordable" area. Don't get me wrong, you still need a fair amount of discretionary income but you won't see 4 and 5 digit price tags in this area.

Whether you purchase an ornament or a diamond, strutting out of Tiffany's with your little blue bag in tow is liberating!

Supplies: Beautiful short cocktail glass, cocktail ring

Playlist: *Watch* - "Breakfast at Tiffany's"

Ingredients

1 ½ ounces Bacardi white rum
½ ounce Malibu rum
½ ounce Blue Curacao
½ ounce fresh lime juice

Soda water
White orchid garnish (optional)

Fill cocktail glass with ice. Add remaining ingredients and top with soda water. Stir gently with a bar spoon, garnish with a white orchid and enjoy.

"Jewelry takes people's minds off your wrinkles"

-unknown

Pitcher Drinks

Sangria-"ish"

This is the ultimate Pitcher drink. I've never liked traditional Sangria so I was motivated to create one that I would enjoy drinking as well as be proud to serve my friends. The drink has an amazing flavor profile and has a beautiful pink hue to it. (I think anything pink is awesome)

Be warned. This drink will creep up on you faster than a cheap pair of panties!

Playlist: "Coconut Water" - Robert Mitchum

Supplies: Large pitcher or jar for infusing (I like using the drink jars with spigot attached)

Ingredients

1 750L bottle of merlot
1 Fifth bottle light rum
3 cups guava nectar
3 cups pineapple juice
4 cinnamon sticks
Pineapple chunks
1 orange cut into thick rounds

Combine all ingredients in large jar or pitcher, stir and let stand in the refrigerator overnight.

When ready to serve, fill tall glasses w/ice, pour in sangria mix and garnish with a "drunken pineapple chunk" from bottom of pitcher.

Girlfriend to Girlfriend tip: Be prepared to start handing out recipe cards after this one!

Summertime

When you live in a place like Portland and it rains what seems like 70% of the time, you're ready for a little vitamin D when it finally hits.

The weather man usually throws us a bone a couple days in March, a teaser in May, and sometime in June we start picking up momentum and feeling some heat.

Nothing feels better than a sun kissed face, fresh pedicure and an outdoor party with friends. People are happier when it's sunny!

Playlist: "Summertime" – DJ Jazzy Jeff & The Fresh Prince

Supplies: Large pitcher, tall glasses, edible flowers

Ingredients

3 cups vodka
4 cups unsweetened pineapple juice
1 cup crème of coconut (Coco Loco)
Slices from (1) medium orange

Combine all ingredients in a pitcher, whisk well and serve over ice in tall glasses. Float edible flower on top.

Peachy Queen

I'm not a big fan of blender drinks. They seem impersonal, and, I don't enjoy the brain freeze that usually goes along with them. I do however, love this little whirled up beauty. So if you're looking for an easy crowd pleaser this summer, this will most certainly do the job!

Playlist: "Georgia on My Mind" – Ray Charles

Supplies: Blender, glasses, cute straws

Ingredients

1 cup fresh squeezed orange juice
8 ice cubes
4 ounces peach schnapps
2 scoops vanilla bean ice cream (good quality)
4 ounces premium vodka
1 fresh peach, sliced

Blend orange juice, ice cubes, peach schnapps and vodka in a blender until the ice cubes are crushed. Add the ice cream and blend until frothy (about 20 seconds). Pour into chilled glasses and garnish with a fresh peach slice.

Serves 4

Velvet Swizzle

Every time I make this drink I feel like I should be poolside at some celebrity birthday bash. This drink has an exotic flavor profile and, is visually appealing to boot!

It calls for Velvet Falernum Liqueur, which has an almond and clove essence that is very unique.

Playlist: "Black Velvet "– Alannah Myles

Supplies: Glass pitcher, swizzle sticks and edible flowers

Note: edible flowers like pansy or nasturtium can be found at most gourmet markets.

Ingredients

12 ounces silver tequila
12 ounces Velvet Falernum
4 ounces fresh lime juice
3 ounces Cointreau
8 ounces passion juice (I like Bolthouse Farms)

Put all ingredients in pitcher and stir vigorously. Serve over ice and float an edible flower on top.

Girlfriend to Girlfriend tip: Hold onto your skirt sweetheart. This drink is so smooth you won't even taste the alcohol.

Cucumber Sparkler

This cocktail is fresh, fragrant and is the perfect accompaniment with Asian inspired appetizers. Try it with Sushi, lettuce wraps or with an Asian spiced flank steak satay.

Playlist: "Phantom of the Opera" soundtrack

Supplies: Glass bowl, glass pitcher, strainer and 8 rock glasses.

Silk kimono and slippers optional!

Ingredients

26 slices fresh cucumber
18 ounces vodka
5 ounces fresh lime juice
5 ounces simple syrup
10 fresh basil leaves
Chilled soda water

In a glass bowl add cucumbers, basil leaves and vodka. Muddle to release the flavors. Strain mixture into a clean glass pitcher. Add lime juice and simple syrup. Stir to combine.

Pour mixture into 8 ice filled glasses leaving about 2 inches from the top. Finish by adding chilled soda water to each glass. Float a couple thin strips of fresh basil on top and serve.

City of Roses

I live in Portland, Oregon, the acclaimed "City of Roses". Every year I can't wait until the roses are in bloom and I can head up to Washington Park for my little self guided tour of the rose gardens.

It's a great place to re-boot and get inspired. I generally stop by my favorite deli, grab a salad and beverage then set up my virtual office on my favorite bench that overlooks the city.

The color and fragrance of this pitcher full of love reminds me of the rose gardens.

Enjoy!

Play list: "Like Red on a Rose" – Alan Jackson

Supplies: Beautiful glass pitcher and champagne flutes for serving

Ingredients

1 750L good quality Rosé wine
2 cups sparkling lemon soda
1 bag frozen blueberries
½ teaspoon rose water
Lemon twist
Rose petal garnish (optional)

Place frozen blueberries into pitcher. Add remaining ingredients and stir. Let stand for 15 minutes and serve in chilled champagne flutes with a few ice cubes in each glass. Garnish with rose petal and lemon twist.

Jazzy Julep

Once again, I raise my little silver julep glass to the South!   One of my favorite drinks is the classic Mint Julep. When I find a bar that knows exactly how to prepare it, I order one.

The Jazzy Julep is a riff on the classic southern cocktail staple, and is perfect for a crowd. The best part about it is you don't need crushed ice or special glasses.

Your girlfriends are sure to award you the Triple Crown after this one!

Giddy-Up.

Playlist: "My Old Kentucky Home" – the official song of the Kentucky Derby.

Supplies: Glass Pitcher, tall skinny glasses.

Ingredients

¾ cup fresh lemon juice
6 tablespoons simple syrup
3/4 cup packed mint leaves
1¼ cup Makers Mark bourbon

2 10-ounce bottles chilled club soda
8 mint sprigs
8 lemon twists

Put lemon juice, simple syrup and mint leaves in a glass bowl. Muddle mint leaves.   Let stand at room temperature for 20 minutes. Strain into pitcher, add bourbon and club soda. Stir.

Fill 8 glasses with ice and distribute drink mix. Garnish with mint sprig and lemon twist.

Infuse Your Booze

Infuse your booze!

Nothing in life comes easy and crafting the perfect cocktail is no exception.

These drinks take a little longer to make but the end result is knock your socks off worth it!

Infusing spirits is really quite simple but takes a little practice to get just the right flavor profile.

Infusing starts with a base alcohol; vodka is the most common, though gin, light rum and even Blanco tequila can make an outstanding end product.

Using fruits, herbs and certain spices can all lend to a unique base for a special cocktail.

Infusing times will vary based on the ingredients that you use. Less intense flavors may need a week or longer to infuse, while more intense flavors only need a few days.

I recommend tracking your spirits by tasting and making notes every couple days. During this process, store in a cool dark place and shake your mixture a couple times a day.

Once you have the flavor that you like, simply strain out the entire mixture into a clean jar or bottle using either cheese cloth, a paper coffee filter, or my favorite, a gold cone coffee filter.

As with any cooking, once you understand the basic principles, it will be easy for you to play around and create your own specialty spirits.

Store your infusions in the refrigerator.

Get creative and have fun in your very own spirit lab!

(Lab coat optional)…

Drunken Rum

This bad boy stands on its own two feet. No need to mix this with anything else. Just serve over ice and enjoy.

I love this on a warm night on the deck with lots of candle lanterns burning.

Playlist: Anything Bob Marley for this one!

Supplies: XL Pitcher or Jar (I like using a drink jar with spigot attached)

Ingredients

1 gallon dark rum
1 fresh pineapple cut into rings (skin removed)
1 vanilla bean split in half lengthwise

Fill Pitcher or jar with Rum. Split Vanilla bean in half, scrape seeds into mix and drop in. Add peeled fresh pineapple rings, cover tightly and store at room temperature for at least 3 days and up to 5.

Before serving, stir and strain over ice in a small glass. Garnish with a cherry.

Citrus Vodka

Once you see how easy it is to make your own citrus vodka you'll never purchase another one.

Citrus brings a vibrant fresh flavor to the party. It's great in drinks with berries (strawberries, blueberries and raspberries), partners beautifully with herbs (basil, cilantro, thyme or rosemary) and is bright and fresh on its own, such as a vodka martini or vodka soda.

Supplies: Mason jar, masking tape and permanent marker

Infusion time: approximately 3 days (this is strictly a matter of preference)

Ingredients

750L bottle vodka
1 fresh lemon

Slice lemon into wheels and drop in jar. Add Vodka. Secure lid and shake vigorously. Write the date and ingredients used on the masking tape and adhere to the jar.

Store the infusion in a cool dark place for three days. Shake twice a day and start tasting after the second day.

When satisfied with the taste, strain the entire mixture out into a clean bowl or jar using a fine mesh strainer, coffee filter or cheese cloth.

Store your finished product in a bottle or jar with tight fitting lid in the refrigerator for up to a week.

Raspberry Infusion

This recipe uses vodka as your base spirit, however, I've also made it with gin and it's fantastic.

Get creative and have fun experimenting with your own combinations.

Supplies: Mason jar, masking tape and a permanent marker

Infusion time: 3-4 days. (Taste your infusion every other day until satisfied)

Tip: don't be alarmed when you see the raspberries expand in size once they sit in alcohol.

Ingredients

750L bottle of vodka
1 pint fresh washed raspberries

Place raspberries into the jar and fill with vodka. Secure lid and shake vigorously. Write the date and ingredients used on the masking tape and adhere to the jar.

Store the infusion in a cool dark place for three to four days. Shake twice a day and start tasting after the second day.

When you have the flavor you're looking for, strain the entire mixture out into a clean bowl or jar using a fine mesh strainer, coffee filter or cheese cloth.

Store your finished product in a bottle or jar with a tight fitting lid in the refrigerator for up to a week.

Lovely Lavender

Lavender delivers a unique taste to cocktails. Use this infusion to make a lemon drop but replace the citrus or regular vodka with the lavender vodka. For a more subtle lavender taste you may want to use one part regular vodka and one part lavender infused vodka for your cocktail.

Tip: If at any time you would like to dilute the lavender taste, simply add more regular vodka.

Supplies: Mason jar, masking tape and a permanent marker

Ingredients

750L bottle of vodka
2 tablespoons dried lavender flowers

Place dried lavender in Mason jar. Fill with vodka. Secure lid and shake vigorously. Write the date and ingredients used on the masking tape and adhere to the jar.

Store the infusion in a cool dark place for approximately five days. Shake daily.

Start testing your infusion after the third day. Once satisfied, strain the entire mixture into a clean jar or bowl using a fine mesh strainer, cheese cloth or coffee filter.

Store in a clean bottle or jar with a tight fitting lid in the refrigerator for up to one week.

Girlfriend to Girlfriend tip: I love making what I call my French-Tuscan drop with this infusion. I make a lemon drop with lavender infused vodka and add a sprig of muddled rosemary.

Lemongrass-
Ginger Tequila

Lemongrass and Ginger are both mild ingredients and will need a longer infusion time. This combination is subtle, but adds a wonderful hint of flavor to the tequila.

Use this infusion for a unique margarita!

Supplies: Mason jar, masking tape and a permanent marker

Ingredients

750L bottle of blanco tequila
2– 1" pieces of fresh ginger
2 stalks of fresh lemongrass cut into large chunks

Place fresh ginger and lemongrass in a Mason jar. Fill with Blanco tequila. Secure lid and shake vigorously. Write date and ingredients used on the masking tape and adhere to the jar.

Store the infusion in a cool dark place for eight days. Shake daily.

Start testing your infusion after the third day. Once satisfied, strain the entire mixture into a clean jar or bowl using a fine mesh strainer, cheese cloth or coffee filter.

Store in a clean bottle or jar with a tight fitting lid in the refrigerator for up to one week.

Sexy Simple Syrups

Sexy Simple Syrups

Simple syrup is a bar staple. It adds a little sweetness or spice, depending on what you infuse it with.

Simple syrup is the perfect neutralizer for a cocktail. It mellows out a strong base spirit and adds a little one-two punch for the remaining ingredients.

Think of Simple syrup as the perfect kiss good-bye before your drink leaves the bar.

Making homemade simple syrup is easy and fun. Play around with different ingredients and come up with your own concoctions.

Simple syrups make delicious nonalcoholic cocktails as well. Simply add an ounce or two to club soda or fruit juice.

Note: People have asked me the difference between a cocktail that has been made with infused simple syrup vs. a cocktail made with an infused alcohol.

The answer is one will give you a noticeably sweeter flavor and one will taste stronger, giving you just a hint of that flavor.

Basic Simple Syrup

Simple syrup can be made using either a 1-to-1 ratio of sugar and water, or for a thicker syrup and slightly sweeter syrup, use 2 cups sugar to 1 cup water.

I use both versions in this book depending on what cocktail I'm making. For some I prefer the thicker version because I like the consistency.

Experiment with both and see which you prefer!

Basic Simple Syrup

1 cup sugar
1 cup water

In a small saucepan combine the sugar and water and bring to a boil, stirring until the sugar is completely dissolved. Immediately remove from heat and let cool completely at room temperature. (Do not overcook)

Pour into a glass jar with tight fitting lid and refrigerate up to two weeks.

Thicker Simple Syrup

2 cups sugar
1 cups water

***Follow the same directions from above**

Lavender Flower Syrup

Lavender brings a lovely smoothness to a cocktail! You won't need as much of this in your cocktail as you would if you were using plain simple syrup. Play around with this one! You're gonna love it in bourbon, vodka and gin based cocktails.

Ingredients

2 cups sugar
1 cup water
2 tablespoons dried lavender
(Lavender can be found in the spice section of your grocery store)

Bring sugar and water to a boil. Stir until sugar dissolves and immediately remove from burner. Stir in lavender and let cool completely at room temperature. Strain cooled syrup through a fine sieve into a clean airtight bottle or jar. Refrigerate until needed, up to 3 weeks. (If it lasts that long)

Lavender Martini

Now that you have this fabulous jar of Lavender Flower Simple Syrup, try it out on these two cocktails!

Ingredients

2 ounces Bombay Sapphire gin
½ once lavender simple syrup
½ ounce dry vermouth
2 dashes orange bitters

Fill shaker with ice. Add remaining ingredients and shake until cold. Strain into a well chilled martini glass.

Chipotle Lime

Use this syrup anytime you want to bring a little sweet heat to the party! It's especially complimentary with tequila, vodka and white rum drinks. I've even put a little dash in a Bloody Mary just to kick things up a notch.

Ingredients

¼ teaspoon chipotle Chile powder
2 cups sugar
1 cup water
1 ¼ cups fresh lime juice (about 9 juicy limes)

In a small saucepan, combine Chile powder, sugar and water. Bring to a boil and stir until sugar dissolves. Immediately remove from heat and let cool at room temperature. Stir in the lime juice.

Pour into a clean jar or bottle with tight fitting lid. Refrigerate until ready to use.

Orange-Rita

You can pretty much start writing me my thank you card now. I have mad love for the classic Margarita, but this one is like Ms. Margarita had a head on collision with a spice wagon!

It's so delicious and packs just enough heat you won't mind that it has less sugar than her predecessor.

Don't be a cry baby. Give it a try before pooh-poohing it. (The heat's not gonna hurt you).

Playlist: "On the Floor" - Jennifer Lopez

Supplies: Shaker and beautiful margarita glass. Big hoop earrings and red lipstick optional.

(Orange-ya' glad you tried it?)

Ingredients

3 ounces Corzo tequila reposado (or other premium tequila)
2 ½ ounce chipotle lime simple syrup (previous page)
½ ounce Cointreau
Lime wedge

Fill shaker with ice. Squeeze the lime wedge into the shaker and drop in. Add remaining ingredients. Shake like it's a maraca and pour into a big margarita or rocks glass. Garnish with a lime wheel or pretty flower.

Simply Vanilla Syrup

Vanilla has such a lovely smooth character I just love using it in cocktails.

Use this syrup in lieu of regular simple syrup when making your next cocktail for another layer of flavor. Experiment around and have fun!

Ingredients

1 cup water
1 cup sugar
2 vanilla beans

In small sauce pan, bring sugar and water to boil. Stir constantly until sugar dissolves. Do not burn.

Immediately remove from heat and add two vanilla beans cut lengthwise, including the seeds (scrape directly into pan).

Let cool for 8 hours. Strain into a clean jar with airtight lid. Refrigerate until ready to use.

Vanhattan

This cocktail is a riff on the classic Manhattan. I proudly refer to it as a *"Vanhattan"* due to the vanilla simple syrup that's in it.

Playlist: "Friends" – Will Smith

Supplies: Shaker, martini glass

Ingredients

3 ounces Makers Mark bourbon
1 ounce sweet vermouth
½ ounce simply vanilla simple syrup* (recipe on previous page)
2 Dashes Angostura bitters

Chill martini glass while prepping. In shaker filled with ice combine all ingredients and stir well with a bar spoon. (Do not shake)

Strain into chilled martini glass and garnish with a cherry.

Basil Syrup

Ingredients

1 cup sugar
1 cup water
½ cup loosely packed fresh basil leaves

In a small saucepan combine the sugar and water and bring to a boil, stirring until the sugar is completely dissolved. Immediately remove from heat, add the fresh basil leaves and let stand at room temperature for 6-8 hours.

Strain into a glass jar with tight fitting lid and refrigerate up to two weeks.

Basil Beauty

Basil is my favorite herb and lucky for me, it rocks in cocktails! In this cocktail I use gin, but it's lovely in vodka as well.

Playlist: "Wannabe" – Spice Girls

Supplies: Shaker, martini glass and muddler

Ingredients

2 ounces premium gin
1 ounce basil syrup* (see previous page)
3 fresh raspberries
1 ounce fresh lime juice

Fill shaker with ice. Drop in fresh raspberries and muddle gently. Add remaining ingredients and strain into a well chilled martini glass. Garnish with a fresh basil leaf.

Girlfriend to Girlfriend tip: Wearing a black sheath dress and a fabulous pair of cheetah print pumps heightens the awesomeness factor of this drink!

Celebration Drinks

Celebration Drinks

I need very few reasons to celebrate. Ever since I was a little girl I love to have fun and be around friends.

My mom says she needs a nap after talking with me on the phone. My friends ask if I ever just want to do "nothing". Here's what happens when I try to do nothing...

Stay with me. It's Saturday morning and I'm sitting on the couch with a cup of coffee. I start getting fidgety, so I head to the bathroom to get a bottle of nail polish to do my nails. On the way to the bathroom, I spot a recent copy of Bon Appétit magazine that I haven't read yet.

I put my manicure on hold and sit back down with the magazine. About half way through (that's about what it takes to get through all the advertising these days), I hit the feature recipe section. Now I'm in *the* zone! I get up, get a pen and paper and start taking notes. Suddenly, I get the itch. I yell down stairs to my husband who has no problem just doing nothing on a Saturday morning. I say "Hey, do you want to have a dinner party?" He yells back "when". "Tonight", I reply. (Duh!)

Suddenly, our lazy Saturday morning goes into high gear. I dump my coffee into a travel mug, pull my hair back in a pony tail and we're off to the market.

The market leads to the flower stand, the flower stand leads to the liquor store and the liquor store leads to a specialty market for edible flowers.

We get back home and I decide to get my inner "Martha Stewart" on. I start playing around with different table setting ideas, some minor re-arranging in the living room and then I drag out some dishes I haven't used in a while. One thing leads to another, and now I'm fussing over glassware until my husband walks in and says "shouldn't we start cooking?"

We work great in the kitchen together. He's the lead slicer-dicer, and I dive right into cooking mode. The sooner we get the prep done, the sooner I can focus on fine tuning my party. Music selection, refilling the candles and setting up the bar!

My goal is to get as much done ahead of time so we can relax and enjoy our guests when they arrive.

I don't believe you need to wait for a reason to celebrate. Hell, I've thrown a party just because I wanted to wear a new pair of shoes.

In this chapter I share with you some of my favorite drinks and the memories that I have while drinking them.

Here's my motto; *"life's short, celebrate often!"*

The Power Suit Story

I created this drink in memory of what I call, my "big break" into Corporate America.

Many years ago when I was working as a consumer loan officer in downtown Portland, I was "discovered" by one of our vendors. I'll call him Bob (*because that's his name*). Bob was in my office one afternoon and said the company he worked for wanted to recruit me.

Initially, he caught me off guard. But then, the more he told me, the more I became interested. (Especially, when he got to the part about a company car and some other sweet perks).

Later that afternoon Bob called and said they wanted to schedule me for a panel interview. I was so excited, that after work I walked up to Nordstrom and purchased what I later would refer to as my "power suit".

It was a designer label, red pencil skirt with a perfectly tailored blazer. It looked amazing and definitely felt more business and less bank-y!

My interview was like "Meet the Fockers", but instead, meet the President, the Vice President and the Sales Manager. Inside I was nervous. Up to that point I had never been through a panel interview process.

The interview lasted about an hour and a half. The President asked me to sell him his wrist watch. The Vice President gave me scenario after scenario asking how I'd handle each one of them. The Sales Manager used sports analogies for just about everything.

I left feeling mentally exhausted! All I could think about was how much I paid for my suit and that it had damn well better been worth it.

The next few days were pure agony! Every time my phone rang I'd practically tip over my pencil cup trying to answer it as fast as I could.

Four days later I got the job and my first paycheck paid off my suit!

Power Suit

Playlist: "The Power" – Snap

Supplies: shaker, martini glass and a current resume! *(Ya never know...)*

Ingredients

2 ounces gin
1 ounce cranberry juice
1/2 ounce simple syrup
½ fresh lime

Fill shaker with ice. Add gin, cranberry juice, simple syrup and juice from the lime. Shake until cold and strain into a well chilled martini glass. Garnish with a lemon twist.

"Dress for the job you want, not the job you have"

The Golden Gate

In the early 90's I accepted a job offer and moved to San Francisco. It was a big move for me. I was young, single and by comparison, from a small town.

I remember having lunch with my dad when I first got the job offer. I told him that the only reason why I *wouldn't* take the job is that I didn't want to move that far from them. (My parents)

In true dad fashion he said, "Karen, I'll always be your dad, but you won't always have this opportunity". Thanks daddy-o!

The first cocktail I had as a new resident of San Francisco was at a cool bar in the financial district where I worked. It was ultra hip, full of pin stripe suits, Monte Blanc pens and smelled like expensive cologne.

It appeared that everyone had money and came from the same gorgeous gene pool.

Anyway, back to the drink. It was a fancy bubbly drink with a beautiful nose to it. It also came with a lot of attitude. (*Seemed to be a trend there*).

Playlist: Sittin' On the Dock of the Bay –Otis Redding

Supplies: champagne flute

Ingredients

4 ounces chilled Prosecco
1 1/2 ounces fresh grapefruit juice
1 ounce Grand Marnier
2 dashes rose water (don't leave this out)

Fill champagne flute with grapefruit juice, Grand Marnier and rose water. Finish with the Prosecco.

Girlfriend to Girlfriend tip: When opportunity knocks, answer!

Soul Sister

This drink reminds me of the South. I was in Atlanta, Georgia staying at this hip hotel while on a buying trip when I experienced this drink.

After ten plus hours of power shopping and spending money like it was going out of style, it was time for a break. I secured a table for one at the hotel bar and ordered this amazing cocktail.

I don't think I would have ordered it if it weren't for me rubbernecking over at the table next to me and seeing this beautiful pink hued cocktail in a funky glass. I asked my waiter what "*she*" was drinking and he said "girrrl, that's our most popular cocktail". Sold! I'll take one. Not only did he turn the word *girl* into a three syllable word, but said if I didn't absolutely love it he'd buy it for me.

Who was I to turn down a cocktail that came with a money back guarantee? He was right. The only thing I needed at this point was another one.

When I got back home I spent the next several weeks trying to recreate it. (Thanks cute bar guy in Atlanta!)

Playlist: "Soul Sister" – Lady Marmalade

Supplies: Fun girlfriends to drink it with, pretty glassware, Shaker

Ingredients

3 ounces strong black tea (preferably home brewed)
2 ounces Makers Mark bourbon
½ ounce simple syrup
3 fresh raspberries
Juice of ½ medium orange

Fill shaker with ice. Drop in raspberries and muddle. Add juice from the orange add remaining ingredients. Shake like there's no tomorrow and strain into a glass filled with ice. Garnish with a fresh mint leaf.

New York Bliss

I was in New York City on another buying trip, but this time I went two days earlier so I could take in a little Manhattan shopping, theatre and some site seeing.

Shortly after landing it started to snow. For the next several days New York was covered! At first I was bummed because it made getting around pretty tough, things were delayed and people were cranky.

But thanks to the snow, I was able to secure incredible, last minute seats to Phantom of the Opera (one of my all time favorites), I got a spa appointment last minute at one of my favorite spa's (Bliss), and then, I was at dinner that night when a group of Japanese business men sent me over a glass of Opus One wine. OMG! I was on a roll.

A day like that deserves a champagne cocktail and that is exactly what I had the next morning at breakfast.

Playlist: "Empire State Of Mind" – Jay Z/Alicia Keys

Supplies: Champagne flute & a sugar cube

Ingredients

1 sugar cube
1 ounce Aperol (an Italian bitter-orange aperitif)
¼ ounce Solerno blood orange liqueur
3 ½ - 4 ounces Prosecco (chilled)
Lemon twist

Fill the flute with Prosecco, and then add the Aperol and Solerno liqueur. Right before serving add the sugar cube. This creates a lovely little bubble show in the glass.

The back story of "The Las Vegas Letter"

None of my travels are without some type of memory, drama or celebration. This trip had it all.

I'll start with the drama. I was in the thick of dealing with a lying, cheating spouse and a very busy business. My life didn't seem like mine. It was more like a made for TV movie or something.

In definite need of a break, I booked an impromptu trip to Las Vegas (alone) so I could do a little thinking.

The first night sucked. I felt like the ONLY person in Las Vegas without a spouse. Obviously that was not the case, but that's what it felt like.

By morning I was energized and felt pretty good. I had a long workout, got a facial and then spent the afternoon at the pool. All of a sudden I decided to write him a letter.

After writing it all down, I felt way better and decided to make the best of the rest of the trip.

I went back to the hotel room, showered, got all dressed up and decided to do a little shopping!

First up, Tiffany & Co. I bought myself a necklace, had it all wrapped up in the coveted blue box and I was off and running. Next stop was Fashion Show Mall and Neiman Marcus. Beautiful store, way too expensive, but who was I to stop when I was just getting started.

I bought two pairs of shoes, a purse and some Yves St. Laurent lipstick. All this power shopping was making me light headed and thirsty.

I took about a 30 minute time out to re-hydrate and fuel up on a light snack before ramping back up. The nice thing about Las Vegas is you can pretty much shop all night.

Flanked with shopping bags, I headed down the strip towards the hotel, but not quite ready to call it a night.

In passing through the casino on the way to more shopping, I thought I'd try my luck on a few slot machines. Though I was having poor luck in my personal life, I felt pretty lucky holding all my awesome purchases, so I put 20 bucks in the machine and after a few pulls, it was cha-ching baby!

I think I ended up winning just over $100.00. Not a bad return on my 20 investment. I quickly cashed out, turned my voucher over for shopping cash and I was back in the saddle.

I think by the time it was all said and done, I ended up with another pair of shoes and some cool earrings.

146

So despite the shit storm I was dealing with at home, I ended up having a great trip, I came back with a new attitude, and, it gave me a delicious drink recipe and another story to share with you for my book, eh?

Have you ever gone on a trip by yourself? I must admit, it is pretty fun. There's no negotiating, the answer is always yes, and, you can dink around in the bathroom getting ready as long as you want.

The Las Vegas Letter

Playlist: "My Way" – Frank Sinatra

Supplies: Martini glass, shaker

*being surrounded by shopping bags heightens the experience!

(Trust me on this one)

Ingredients

3 ounces prepared lemonade
2 ounces vodka
3 fresh strawberries
4 mint leaves

Fill shaker with ice. Drop in strawberries and mint leaves. Muddle well. Add lemonade and vodka. Shake, strain and pour into a well chilled martini glass. Garnish with a lemon twist.

Girlfriend to Girlfriend tip: Even if you never send that certain someone the letter you wrote (though I personally hand delivered it), it *will* make you see things much clearer.

P.S. Having an excuse to shop with reckless abandonment is frick-in' amazing! LOL

Northwest Drop

This drink celebrates all the wonderful memories of visiting my Dad in Hood River, Oregon. In the fall we would drive what is called the "historic fruit loop". It's a beautiful drive in the country where we would purchase Hood River apples to make pie or just bite into one on the ride home.

I can't remember one single trip that it wasn't sunny and clear. Once in a while we'd stop at one of the road side stands and share a slice of fresh apple pie while sitting at an old picnic table. I miss those drives with my dad!

Playlist: "Letters from Home" – Scotty McCreery

Supplies: Shaker, pretty goblet

Ingredients

2 ounces brandy
1 ounce light rum
3 ounces apple juice
½ ounce fresh lemon juice
½ ounce Myers dark rum

Fill shaker with ice. Pour remaining ingredients except the dark rum. Shake briefly and strain into a well chilled goblet. Just before serving "float" dark rum on top. Garnish with a thin apple slice.

"Suite" Dreams
The memory behind the drink

I can't count how many times I've been to Dallas, Texas for business, but every single time was sensational.

One trip did make the epic hall of fame! I was going for 7 nights but had to split it between two hotels. The first hotel was downtown Dallas. When I got there, the reservation agent didn't have record of my stay. She then proceeded to tell me they were booked for the week.

I took a deep breath, refrained from going ape shit, and asked for the manager. After he made several visits to the back room, he came back and said they had one room left. The Grand Suite. (*Oh, that's too bad!*). He made every attempt to negotiate with me on the price. I smiled and told him based on the circumstance I wasn't willing to pay anymore than the original room I was booked for.

Within a few moments, he handed me a giant, old school brass key and told me to have a wonderful stay.

Unbeknownst to me, my world was about to change. (At least for 4 days)

I opened the door to my Suite and for a moment, thought they accidently sent me to a ballroom! This mother was completely tricked out. Three bedrooms, four bathrooms, beautiful living room, kitchen, formal dining room with a giant gilded chandelier, two patios with outdoor furniture and, a magnificent view of downtown Dallas.

I didn't want to leave this place! I slept in a different room each night, ordered room service and skipped the first day of my buying trip so I could chill on the patio.

It was time to check-out and head over to my second hotel of the week. Of course I was in a tiny little funk, as I was leaving paradise, but at the same time I was excited to check out my next set of digs.

I had read a lot about this next hotel, as it had been getting a lot of hype around town. It was a swanky boutique hotel that had recently opened.

On the taxi ride over I remember the driver saying "don't be surprised if you see a celebrity or two".

About that time he pulled in and I thought to myself, "how could this trip get any better". The front of the hotel looked like an exotic car lot. Each car perfectly parked in a semi circle. Lamborghini, Bentley, Mercedes, and I'm sure there was an Austin Martin or two.

When I first walked in, I didn't know if I was in a club, an art gallery or a hotel. It was the perfect mix of hip, luxe and whimsy.

The rooms were sleek, modern and sexy.

The service was impeccable. It was like they had a GPS tracking device on me! I would leave my room and some hot guy would be at the elevator waiting to help me.

I'd get back to my room only to find candles burning and hip music playing in the background. Every night they would leave a clever message or a quote on my pillow, (printed on beautiful paper) and some kind of old school candy. One night they left Pop Rocks, another night a PEZ dispenser and so on.

The first night I realized I left my tooth brush at the last hotel. I went down to the lobby simply to see if they had one for purchase, and within moments I was on my way to a local convenience store in their big black Escalade courtesy car.

Traveling alone may not seem like fun, but take it from me, it may very well give you an experience, (or two) of a lifetime!

Thank you Dallas!

"Suite Dreams"

"Suite" Dreams

So now you know the story behind this next drink! I don't why, but at home, I pretty much never go to a bar alone, yet when I'm traveling, I actually look forward to it.

I don't look at it as a pick-up place. I look at it as a safe place to go to have dinner for one. (BTW, I'm not talking "club", I'm talking about a classy restaurant with a bar attached). It doesn't seem weird to me at all to saddle up to the bar, order dinner and a drink, and just relax after a busy day. I seem to get excellent service and something magic happens when the bartender finds out you're traveling alone. All of a sudden it's as if they take you under their wing and give you VIP treatment.

Here's to you Hotel ZaZa!—thanks for making my trip "Za-best" ever & for the inspiration behind this cocktail. (X + O)

Playlist: "Mr. Boombastic" - Shaggy

Supplies: shaker, martini glass, muddler

Ingredients

2 ounces premium vodka
2 thin slices Jalapeno pepper (no seeds)

1 ounce Peach Schnapps
1 lime wedge
3 ounces fresh squeezed orange juice

Fill shaker with ice. Drop in the jalapeno pepper, squeeze juice from the lime and drop in. Muddle the pepper and lime. Add the remaining liquids. Shake well, strain and pour into a well chilled martini glass.

Girlfriend to Girlfriend tip: If you find yourself on a solo trip, don't fall prey to your hotel room! Get out and circulate.

The Skyy's The Limit

I moved to San Francisco about the same time Skyy Vodka launched onto the scene.

I was invited to their launch party at Armani Exchange in the City. I remembered how cool it was seeing those signature cobalt blue bottles all lined up!

It was a great event and at the end they handed out some swag, including little blue shot glasses. (*I still have mine*).

Those two years were amazing. I felt so fortunate to be working for a great company and living in such an incredible city that I thought the perfect name for this cocktail would be "The Skyy's The Limit".

Enjoy!

Playlist: "Strangers in the Night" – Frank Sinatra

Supplies: shaker, martini glass, muddler

Ingredients

2 ounces Skyy Vodka
½ ounce fresh lemon juice
½ sprig fresh rosemary
½ ounce simple syrup
5 blackberries
Float of chilled Prosecco (Italian sparkling wine)

Fill shaker with ice. Drop in blackberries and rosemary sprig and muddle gently. Add vodka, lemon juice and simple syrup. Shake until cold and strain into a well chilled martini glass with a fine strainer. Float the chilled Prosecco on top and serve. Garnish with a sprig of rosemary.

Brunch Cocktails

High Maintenance

I love having friends over for brunch. It's a nice change of pace from a formal dinner party and it's a perfect excuse for me to break out my feminine linens and fancy glassware.

Brunch to me just screams bubbly, flowers, candles and tea cups.

The next time you have the itch to entertain, why not host a brunch?

Playlist: "The Girl from Ipanema" – Stan Getz

Supplies: Glass Pitcher, champagne glasses

Serves 8

Ingredients

750L bottle sparkling pink champagne, chilled
2 Cups red fruit punch, chilled
2 Cups white grape juice, chilled
2 Cups pineapple juice (unsweetened), chilled

Pour all ingredients into a glass pitcher, stir and serve immediately.

Morning Glory

I love it when I get a good night's sleep and I wake up smiling! Even better when it's sunny outside and the birds are chirping.

Its mornings like these that make hanging out on the deck absolutely wonderful.

Playlist: "Your Smiling Face" – James Taylor

Supplies: Heat proof mugs for serving

Serves 4

Ingredients

750L Bottle red wine (Beaujolais or Merlot)
1 Cup Apple juice
½ Cup sugar
3 tablespoons mulling spices

In heavy sauce pan, bring all ingredients to a boil. Reduce heat and simmer 15-20 minutes. Strain through a fine strainer into a clean pan.

Ladle into small tempered glass mugs. Serve hot.

Mimosa-y

I can appreciate a classic Mimosa, but I refuse to drink a cheap one. You know what I'm talking about. The $3.00 special, the bottom-less pitcher or the ones included at a cheap Sunday brunch.

They're made with crap champagne and fake orange juice. No wonder people say Champagne gives them a headache!

I like my Mimosa's with a twist. You be the judge.

Playlist: Anything "Diana Krall"

Supplies: Glass pitcher, champagne glasses

Ingredients

750L bottle dry white wine, chilled
1 cup fresh squeezed orange juice (strained)
¼ cup Grand Marnier
1 ½ cups sparkling water, chilled
Thin cut orange slices for garnish

Stir all ingredients together in a glass pitcher. Serve immediately.

Girlfriend to Girlfriend tip: Invite your girlfriends over on a Saturday morning for a Mimosa bar. Set up a beautiful arrangement of glasses, fruit, herbs, a variety of champagne and juices. Let your guest get creative and customize their own signature Mimosa.

Maui Sunrise

My husband and I never get sick of visiting Maui, Hawaii. I love how laid back it is and how the natives have so much respect for their land.

The sunsets, fragrant flowers and white sandy beaches are all part of why we love it.

This drink reminds me of a cocktail I had at the Four Seasons in Wailea, on the south side of Maui, Hawaii.

Playlist: "Blue Hawaii" – Elvis Presley

Supplies: Shaker, low ball glass

Ingredients

2 ounces Malibu rum
½ ounce orange Curacao
½ ounce almond syrup (like Monin)
¾ ounce lime juice (fresh squeezed)
½ ounce dark rum
Garnish with fresh mint sprig

Combine all ingredients, except dark rum in shaker filled with ice. Pour into a low ball glass filled with crushed ice. Top with dark rum, garnish with mint sprig and serve.

Girlfriend to Girlfriend tip: This will undeniably be a brunch favorite with your girls! I am telling you right now, these drinks are a little island treasure in cup. Be prepared for your girlfriends to start chanting Mahalo!

P.S. This drink tastes way better in flip-flops and a sundress.

Kiki's Gin Fizz

I have to admit, the first time I ever had a gin fizz I didn't like it at all. I felt compelled to drink it, as I was at a fancy schmancy outdoor garden party at a beautiful estate.

Around my fourth or fifth sippy-poo my palette and I got on the same page and I liked it.

I asked the hostess for her recipe and she said in a polite-bitchy way, (I call that being "pitch-y"), "I'm sorry, it's a family recipe". *(Whatever, I'll figure it out).*

So off I go, into my drink lab again to create this little gem. It rocks, if I don't say so myself.

Playlist: "Somebody That I Used To Know" - Gotye

Supplies: Blender, pretty short goblets or rock glasses

Makes 3 drinks

Ingredients

¼ cup heavy cream
¼ cup milk

Juice of 1 whole lemon
5 Teaspoons sugar (regular)
1 Tablespoon vanilla extract
½ Teaspoons flower water (this is critical)
5 ounces Bombay Sapphire gin
Nutmeg
Ice

Fill the blender half way up with ice. Add all ingredients, except for the nutmeg and puree until frothy. Taste and make adjustments if necessary.

Pour into glasses and top with a light dusting of fresh nutmeg. *(This is paramount to the flavor of this drink).*

Enjoy my lovelies!

Bright Eyed and Bushy Tailed

I have very curly, thick hair and when I wake up I've got a full head of Medusa like curls with a mind of their own.

The curls have to be patient, because this early my mind is on one thing and one thing only and that's a strong cup-o-Joe.

I'm pretty serious about my morning coffee. I don't like coffee with breakfast just straight up, first thing.

This cocktail is the perfect mid morning nudge for a brunch. Assuming you've already had your "real" coffee, this will be a welcome treat with your girlfriends.

Playlist: anything "Norah Jones" is perfect for a lazy morning with friends

Ingredients

1 mug extra strong hot coffee or espresso
1 ounce Cointreau
Whipped cream

Cinnamon
Orange zest

In a hot cup of coffee add the Cointreau. Add whipped cream, sprinkle of cinnamon and a dash of fresh orange zest on top.

Girlfriend to Girlfriend tip: Take a little hiatus from the morning grind. Grab a stack of gossip magazines, a dark pair of sunglasses and a flakey croissant!

It doesn't get any better than this sister!

The Fainting Couch

(You'll need one after this drink)

When I was little I was fascinated by the velvet, one armed chaise lounge called "the fainting couch". I never understood why they were always "off limits" to actually use. Maybe that was part of the fascination.

Playlist: A Sunday Kind of Love – Etta James

Supplies: Tall cocktail glass and perhaps a silk sleeping mask for your eyes while you rest!

Ingredients

1 ounce fresh lime juice
1 ounce fresh lemon juice
1 ounce pineapple juice (unsweetened)
1 ¼ ounce dark rum
1 ¼ ounce white rum
½ ounce Malibu rum

In shaker filled with ice combine all ingredients and pour into a tall cocktail glass.

"My nerves could use a drink"

- *Grace Kelly, To Catch a Thief*

Party 101

Tips for a successful party

What's in a name? A lot actually. Think about some of the invitations you've received over the years. What was the party called? An event, celebration, fête, bash, shindig or soiree? All of them get the message across, but each one has a different feel.

When I get invited to a soiree, I start thinking black dress and cocktails, but when someone invites me to a bash I think keg, bbq and hard rock.

If I'm invited to an "Event", I can't wait. If someone uses the term fête, I assume they're either a. French or b. having a classy party with lots of bubbles!

A successful party takes thought, planning and execution. After that all you need is some good friends to share it with.

It wasn't until I started entertaining that I could fully appreciate the hard work and effort that went into all the parties that I had attended.

I believe learning how to entertain makes you a better guest. I also learned how important it is to know your guests before inviting them to your house.

One of my girlfriends asked me if I ever had a bad party. Actually, I've had a few. The first was a dinner party where the guests had no manners, the second was a "Jerry Springer" moment and the third was just weird.

My husband and I invited three couples over for dinner. We always ask (especially if it's someone we don't know very well) if they have anything they can't eat or are allergic to.

Apparently these people thought they were going to a restaurant. One girl said she was vegetarian but will eat fish.

The second guest said she hates fish, but likes lobster and steak. The third guest requested chicken because she hates seafood and steak.

She actually showed up with a frozen Jenny Craig meal "just in case" she didn't like what we were fixing. (*What the hell!*)

That was the first time I ever prepared 3 different entrees for a dinner party and the last time I ever prepared dinner for those people.

The "Jerry Springer" moment was when we had another couple over for some wine tasting. The couple started bickering, then fighting, then yelling and finally, the grand finale.....He said something about the shirt she was wearing and that totally pissed her off so she removed it and threw it at him. So now, I had a half naked girl in my living room sitting on the couch pouting.

I couldn't take anymore of her childish BS, so I asked her to leave.

She did. Without her shirt and I haven't seen her since.

Finally, the weird-o's. This couple showed up two hours late for our dinner party, drunk off their asses and then started going through our cabinets asking what else we had to drink. As if that wasn't weird enough, they excused themselves to go outside and smoke a cigarette right in the middle of dinner.

Unbeknown to me, they had brought their dog with them. When I looked out the window to see where they were, I saw them sitting in our driveway in the back of their SUV smoking their cig while the dog was having his way with our flowerbeds.

So there you have it. You're going to have a few mishaps. That's just part of the ride. But it does make for some good laughs at your next dinner party!

Entertaining on any level is work. It's a time commitment, financial commitment and it requires planning down to the smallest of details. The payoff is seeing your guests have fun, laugh and enjoy themselves.

When I'm in the mood to entertain, I break it down into three parts. I call it my "T.P.E" plan. (Think, Plan, Execute).

If you follow these simple steps you'll stay focused, inspired and on task.

Think

- ✓ What kind of party do I want to have? Is it a special occasion or just because.

- ✓ The menu. Is it going to be a dinner party, cocktails and appetizers or wine and cheese tasting?

- ✓ Do I want a sit down party or an informal mixer? Plan your menu accordingly! (Nobody wants to stand up and eat spaghetti)

✓ Guest list (how many people, girls night, couples)

✓ What time is my party? Rule of thumb is if you have people over during "normal" dinner hours, you need to serve dinner. At the very least, serve heavy appetizers/tapas.

✓ Invitations. How will I let my guest know of my party? If it's casual and last minute a simple text or phone call may be all that is necessary. If you're celebrating something special, a written invite with advance notice is appropriate. For a larger party, you may want to utilize an electronic invitation service such as evite.com

✓ Do I want my guests to bring something? If so, be specific and carefully select who you delegate each dish to. (don't ask the friend that's always late to bring the appetizer and don't ask the friend that doesn't cook to bring a side dish)

✓ What do I want the vibe to be like? (Food, drink, music, table setting) Your guests will appreciate the details.

Plan

✓ Set a budget. Entertaining can be expensive, so figure out ahead of time what you can spend. I've found that a dinner party can actually be less expensive than offering several appetizers.

✓ Finding ways to utilize your ingredients in multiple applications is a great money saving tip. (Buying specialty herbs and spices will add up quickly if you won't be using them for anything else).

✓ Wine is generally more expensive than cocktails. Be prepared for your friends to drink more than you think they would, and they usually go for the nicer stuff when it's available.

✓ Menu planning. Food, weather and time of day can affect your guests' preferences. I like to decide on my main course first (if it's a dinner party) then I design the remainder of my menu.

✓ If you're trying a new recipe, read it over several times so you don't miss any crucial steps when you prepare it for the first time.

✓ Unless you know for sure that your guests are real adventurous, stick with ingredients that most people are familiar with. (Note: For some reason Brussels sprouts are at the top of the do not like list!)

✓ Know your limitations. How much time do you have to prepare, do you have enough space, can you prep ahead of time, do you have enough dishes and flatware for the amount of people you're inviting? (you don't want to have to wash dishes between courses)

✓ People tend to eat less in the summer and more in the winter.

✓ In the summertime people drink more white and sparkling wine than red.

✓ If you're planning on mixing cocktails for more than 6-8 people, consider "batching" the recipe beforehand. *Note:* not all ingredients are good for batching.

✓ Plan on about a pound of ice per person for a cocktail party.

✓ If you're serving a heavy main course, then offer a simple, light appetizer.

✓ If you serve bread with dinner, don't offer bread with your appetizers or your guest will be to full to enjoy your lovely meal!

✓ If you'll be serving a super cheese-y main course, skip offering cheese based dips/spreads for your appetizer.

✓ Create your shopping list by categories and by store (meat, produce, liquor, bakery) this is an efficient way to shop and a huge time saver.

Execute

✓ Create a party punch list and timeline. Completely write out your menu and drinks.

✓ Write down what you can do ahead in the order of priority (make sauces, marinades or dressings, wash and prep produce, make dessert, batch cocktails, chill wine and beer, iron table linens, clean glassware & dishes, set the table, flowers, prep candle holders, music selection and so on. The more you do in advance the less stress you'll have and you will be able to spend more time with your guests.

✓ If you've delegated certain dishes for your guests to bring, confirm that everyone is still a go!

✓ If you have delegated a dish that needs to be either warmed or kept cool, make sure you make room in your refrigerator ahead of time and remember to adjust your own cooking to accommodate the dish that will need to share your stove or oven.

✓ Pre-wash any bowls or platters that your guests may need to display what they brought. (Trust me on this. You will have guests that will bring a sack of groceries to prepare their dish from start to finish at your house, or just simply bring a bag of chips and dip that they purchased on the way over)

✓ Consider renting dishes or glassware for your next party. It's an inexpensive and convenient way to go if you don't own enough glassware or dishes for what you need.

✓ Relax. Have fun. Enjoy your party.

Party Fouls, No-No's & Details

✓ Don't run out of ice (party foul)

✓ Clean your bathroom and any room that your guests will have access to (details)

✓ Have extra T.P. where guest can see it. (party foul)

✓ Have an area for guests to hang their coat and purse (detail)

✓ Select and organize your music ahead of time. Pick an upbeat tempo to kick things off, smooth tunes for dinner and finish with something lively so people don't fall asleep. Instrumental music works well at dinner. (details)

✓ Never burn scented candles at the dinner table. (No-No)

✓ Limit the height of your centerpiece. Your guest shouldn't have to get their inner Gladys Cravitz (*Bewitched*) on by having to peer through the flowers to see who's on the other side. (No-No)

✓ Not everyone is an animal lover! (Especially a cat hanging out on the countertop while you're prepping food/drink). Arrange to have your animal(s) in a separate area for the party. (Party Foul/No-No)

Fun Party Themes for Your Next Event

Finding the time, energy and reason to entertain can be over-whelming, however, having a theme to base your event around makes it super simple and your guests will appreciate it.

By theme, I don't mean turning your house into a casino, a club or a cantina. In fact, I don't recommend it. Instead, pick just enough of a theme that it spurs some creative juices so you can get your party mo-jo going.

Start with your menu. Once you decide on that, it will be easy to integrate little bits and pieces into the rest of your party. This could mean designing your flowers, candles, dishes, music, invitations (if applicable) and your overall "vibe" around what you'll be serving.

I like to envision the look, vibe and feel that I want for my party and then plan my menu. Whether you pick your menu first or your theme first, you will find it to be a great starting point to spur creativity and make the entire process less stressful, more fun and relaxing.

Another advantage of having a basic theme is if you're having your guests contribute, it makes it easy on them to plan their dish or beverage.

It is one thing to be super easy going with a "whatever" attitude, but it can make your guests uncomfortable if you are ill prepared.

Be specific as to what you'll be serving and what you need others to bring. This eliminates duplicate dishes, not enough "real" food and too many chips and cheese dips.

Here's to a fun, frazzle free party!

What are you waiting for? Start planning.

Cheers.

Fun Party Themes for Your Next Event

Tipsy Tapas Night – Have the girls over for small plates and fun cocktails.

Make-up and Margarita's – Call on a local make-up artist in your area and everyone pitch in to have her come over to demonstrate some of the latest make-up tips.

Cupcake and Bubbles Night – Have everyone bring their favorite bottle of bubbles and serve a variety of delicious cupcakes.

Paris Flea Market – Invite your girlfriends over for an indoor swap meet while sipping on French inspired cocktails and appetizers. Ask each person to bring 10-15 things that they would like to "trade" for someone else's treasures.

Christmas Cards and Cocktails - One of those tasks we all put off until the last minute! What better way to get it done than with your girlfriends and festive cocktails.

Wine and Whine Night – Catch up over a glass of wine while passing assorted cheeses, antipasto and some crusty French bread from a local bakery.

Breakfast at Tiffany's - This classic movie never gets old! Invite your friends over for brunch and a movie. Start with a black and white theme, use aqua blue and white as accent colors and sprinkle faux pearls and jewels in the center of your table.

Interactive Pizza Night - Have each person bring a special topping and set up a "mini pizza" bar. Purchase pre-made dough at your local market, make a big salad, break out that heirloom red and white checkered table cloth and serve a big red wine.

Mini Martini Night – Ask each girlfriend to bring a small bottle of her favorite spirit to share (Vodka or Gin). Set up a martini bar with dry and sweet vermouth, a variety of cocktail olives, onions and citrus for making twists. Purchase mini martini glasses at the party store and have fun experimenting.

30 THINGS (OTHER THAN COCKTAILS) THAT WILL LIFT YOUR SPIRIT, BOOST YOUR CONFIDENCE & ROCK YOUR INNER HOTNESS!

1. Give yourself a monthly research project! Cooking, sewing, travel, decorating. Whatever your passion or interest, spend 30 minutes per day and learn more. (Yes, you can make time. Simply limit your FB or Twitter time)

2. Get your eyebrows shaped and waxed. It's one of the most inexpensive beauty enhancers around! If you've never done it, book an appointment today. You won't believe the difference it makes. (just make sure you go to a reputable salon)

3. Invest in a Clarisonic oscillating cleaning machine. (Unlike a snake, you only get one skin, so take care of it) Glow baby glow...

4. Wash your face before bed (Yes, it makes a world of difference)

5. Don't use tanning beds.

6. Try wearing false eyelashes on the outer corner of your eye. (*Go on...you little siren!*)

7. Start a fitness program (sorry, there is no magic pill) Start small and in no time you will notice a tighter bum, flatter tummy and your skin will look amazing from the increased circulation!

8. Water, agua H20! Whatever you call it – drink it. (it's liquid magic for the body)

9. De-Clutter your life. Pick a room a week and start purging, filing and organizing. It will make you feel free!

10. Smile more!

11. Have a professional bra fitting. It's a free service at most specialty and department stores and will make all the difference in how your clothes fit and look.

12. Buy a pair of stilettos. Instant confidence booster!

13. Get in the habit of sending handwritten thank you cards on a regular basis. (yes, snail mail)

14. Throw a party for no reason. No more excuses. Spending time with friends and family is priceless. (the more you do it the easier it gets)

15. Splurge on a spa day! You'll feel totally re-booted, your skin will glow and your soul will feel nourished.

16. Take a time out. Before posting your life story (good/bad) on your Facebook, texting your ex while you're tipsy or sending an email telling a friend what you really think, get up and do something productive for a couple hours. There is no "cyber delete" key. (you'll thank yourself later)

17. Start each day with a list of priorities. It keeps you focused and feels amazing to check things off the list and out of your head.

18. Get a seasonal make-over. Free, at most department stores, salons and specialty stores. It's a great way to keep current on trends, replenish your cosmetics and wear colors that match your seasonal skin tone. (rarely, does the same color palette work year round)

19. Put fresh flowers in your bathroom. It's fun to wake up and see them sitting there! It turns your bathroom into a dressing room.

20. Use your best dishes, stemware and linen napkins every night at the dinner table. Why not? It turns every meal into a special occasion.

21. Splurge! Buy a pair of great fitting jeans. The best fit isn't always the most expensive but shell out as much as you can afford if you find a pair that looks amazing. (You will get more use out of a great pair of jeans than anything else in your closet).

22. Be Nice. Start making a conscious effort to make some-one feel good every day. If a stranger looks nice, tell them. Hold the door open for someone, or, send your hair stylist a thank you card telling her you love your hair. (if you do)

23. Clean your make-up brushes at least once a week with mild soap and water or brush cleaner. It keeps the bacteria in check. (dry them in a cup with the brush end up)

24. Spring for new mascara every month. (If you have to "pump" your mascara to get the color on the wand, toss it) nothing beats fresh, bacteria free mascara.

25. Re-paint your walls. The fastest and least expensive way to update any room is paint! (Instant home improvement)

26. Make a cake from scratch. It's easy and impressive!

27. Treat yourself to a fun new accessory this season. Jewelry is like adding your signature to an outfit.

28. Eat your fruits and vegetables. (Your skin will thank you!)

29. Laugh more. (They say laughing makes us live longer). So does that mean I'll live to be, say, 500?

30. Start making your dreams a reality!

Resources

As the saying goes…It's not WHAT you know it's WHO you know. This holds true in cooking, entertaining, decorating and by all means, making cocktails.

I have included a broad range of resources from dating websites to party supplies and everything in between.

The following resources are strictly my opinion and the opinions of friends that I respect. I do not endorse or benefit from mentioning the following companies. *(Except my own, www.myktini.com)*

Celebrate every day. Live like you mean it!

XO,

KIKI

www.myktini.com

P.S. People always ask me "Kiki, what's your favorite cocktail?" Honey, that's easy. The next one!

Resources

PARTY SUPPLIES & BAR SUPPLIES

Bergreen.com
mistermojito.com
marthastewart.com
potterybarn.com
crateandbarrel.com
layercakeshop.com
krazystraws.com
fishseddy.com

CONFECTIONARY TREATS

ediblegold.com
bedazzlemybonbons.com
magnoliabakery.com
deandeluca.com

JUICE, SYRUPS & PUREE'S

perfectpuree.com
monin.com
jonessoda.com

PAPER & INVITATIONS

paper-source.com
etsy.com
evite.com (online invites)

MUSIC

iTunes.com
spotify.com

HEALTH & BEAUTY

latisse.com (eyelash lengthener)
clarisonic.com (oscillating skin care system)
crunch.com
weightwatchers.com
sephora.com
shape.com

FINANCE

freecreditreport.com
suzeorman.com
amazon.com (order the book **Smart Girls Finish Rich**, David Bach)

INSPIRATION

www.myktini.com (sip, sparkle & laugh)

DÉCOR

designsponge.com
housebeautiful.com
elledecor.com
johnathanadler.com

STYLE

poppin.com (super cute office supplies)
InStyle.com
more.com

DATING WEBSITES

match.com
eharmoney.com

Made in the USA
San Bernardino, CA
16 March 2013